It Takes a Funny Man...

The Best of Bill Berdine

by William C. Berdine
1995

International Standard Book Number 0-9631802-1-5
Library of Congress Catalog Number 94-96825
Printed in the United States of America
Copyright © 1994 by William C. Berdine
Princeton, West Virginia 24740

Published by
Berdine Publishing Company
Princeton, West Virginia

This book is dedicated to all those friends who told me their stories so I could repeat them and take the credit for ingenuity and humor.

And to all those politicians who did all the unbelievable things I write about most. Without those, it would not have been possible.

And last, but certainly not least, to my other half, Margy, who mislead me into thinking that my writing is funny by laughing until the tears rolled.

Bill Berdine

Index

Foreword

This book is a collection of articles from the column, "A View From the Mountain," which is carried weekly in The West Virginia Hillbilly, a weakly publication which is published in Richwood, West Virginia for nationwide distribution.

Some of the articles have appeared in other newspapers which have considerably larger circulatory problems but not nearly the notoriety.

The articles are about everything from fish to nuts, some of which sport two legs while others grow either under- or above-ground.

Some of the articles are political satire, dated by the occurrences about which they were written, but applicable regardless of who the old or new culprits might be.

Some are timeless, although the subject really did happen at some time or another. That means that all are based more or less on fact, which is often funnier than fiction.

The book is not intended to portray any particular individual in any particular light. Except for two or three, that is.

Any reference to any person living, almost living, or past living is purely coincidental. Unless you have already heard the story, too. Then it may or may not be quite so purely.

The articles are not in any particular order. Not alphabetical, not chronological, not subjectical, nor anythingelsical. I typed them just as the copy turned face-up beside the computer.

I did attempt to put in an index, but knowing how disorganized I can be, I wouldn't guarantee that it is in any order either.

What I think is political truth may appear to you as something else entirely. Neither of us can mistake the hillside humor for anything else. Or at least I hope not.

The scribblings are from some of my more recent articles. I would have included some of the older ones, but I seem to have mislaid them.

You may get the idea that I nip only at present politicians in those which are political satire. Not so. I bit the hair of the dog that preceded the present prescence, and, God willing and my ink doesn't freeze, I'll nip at the future prescences--unless we lose our rights under the Constitution because too many of you didn't pay attention to what I was saying.

The articles are in their original form, just as they were written and before I started compressing them to fit my allotted inches. Most of the short ones are those which were written after my assigned inches got shorter by about a half. It is harder to get funny in fourteen inches than in twenty-six.

You will see a couple of articles that appear to be too long for regular newspaper articles. That's because they weren't.

I stuck in a couple of pieces from some of my other writings to take up space and to funny it up a bit. The bad part about those is that they really happened. At least I think they did.

I also stuck in a few of my unbrilliant sayings. You may have thought you almost heard some of them before. If you think you heard them exactly as they are written here, you had better have your ears checked. You've been hearing things. Either that or someone has pilfered my puns before I got them from the paper to the print.

Bill Berdine

What She Was, She Wasn't No Carpenter

I run into some of the most interesting people while selling my book, "The Berdine Un-Theory of Evolution and other Scientific Studies Including Hunting, Fishing, and Sex," which pokes fun at that other work of fiction, The Theory of Evolution.

I contend that the people who try to sell me on the idea that I came from an ape lack two things--a good product and an experienced salesman.

I met a delightful young lady from that city up there on the other end of the state where some of us poor folks pay good money to send our younguns so they can learn to spell and figger better than their parents.

She is Anna Brown (from Morgantown) and I have a sneaking suspicion that she could be almost as funny as I am if she had half a chance. She might even be funnier.

She told me a story about one of her closer relatives who shall remain somewhat anonymous in this account. When she reads it, she'll know that little Annie told.

That female relative and her other half decided to go into the construction business on a temporary basis. That business was designed to build just one house, their own. It eventually included another smaller house out back, but that one was added to the plans after construction was well under way. Sort of like an ell in an architect's plan.

The little one was built only because of the unfore-

1

seen strain on the liquid assets they needed for the big house. They just didn't see their way clear at the time to make the outhouse an inhouse.

The space was there. What was missing from the inhouse was the porcelain appurtenances.

The husband worked diligently to erect the little house in order to have it ready for occupancy in case of a dire emergency.

He dug a hole. He put the floor and joists in proper position over the pit. He put up plywood sides so that every trip would not be a lesson in show and tell for the neighbors and any other strays who might happen to wander by. He even put on a temporary tar-paper roof so the catalog wouldn't get wet.

He nailed the Sears and Roebuck toilet paper to the wall at a convenient height so that one could rip off a page or two without having to leave the comfort of the rough seat.

He put in a fine bench with a nice oak board seat. If his oaks were a mite on the skinny side like most oaks nowadays, he probably spliced a couple narrow ones together to make it wide enough so they wouldn't get splinters in their backs from the plywood behind. It was just the right height for maximum comfort.

And then he must have either mislaid his saw or one of the neighbors borrowed it. Neighbors are like that, especially if they can't afford one of their own.

What he had so masterfully constructed turned out to be a no-holer.

2

His bride of several years nagged and carped at him four or five times a day for nigh on to three weeks. The oak board seat was nice, but it wasn't nearly half as good as a knotty pine board with holes in it. Properly sized and spaced, of course.

One day, no doubt in desperation from that ailment they talk about so much on television at suppertime and suffering from a severe case of bucketitis, she decided to take matters into her own hands.

She searched through her hubby's tool box and pilfered his carpenter's pencil. She marched herself out to the little facility, plopped her broad beam down on the board seat and marked the outline of her posterior parts with the pilfered pencil on the oak board.

She apparently looked somewhere he hadn't because she located his wayward saw. Maybe the neighbor decided he needed to borrow something else.

She sawed away at the self-imposed pattern until she had a suitable (?) hole on her side of the plank. He could cut his own hole when he found the time.

Men are built just a little differently than women. He may not have needed a hole so urgently, especially if he hadn't cut down all the trees to get lumber for the house.

She could hardly wait for the cutout to drop out. She flung the saw into the corner under the nail holding the catalog and pre-peeled to proceed.

That was about the time she learned that some holes can be cut just too blamed big. She hadn't allowed for overlap.

The young lady was a genius, even if she wasn't a full-fledged card-totin' nail bender. She rushed to the five and dime and bought some pretty red and white checked oilcloth and a batt of cotton. She designed a doughnut-shaped cushion, complete with a hole in the middle so the cushion wouldn't interfere with the real purpose of the little shack. She installed it atop the board seat in the most advantageous position.

They wound up with the only little house out back that you had to ride sidesaddle.

And that is a true story.

So help me, Anna Brown.

Never do today what you put off until tomorrow yesterday.

West Virginia is Blessed
With Honest Lawyers

Here I go again, about halfway watching the news on television and punching my remote control buttons in a desperate search trying to find something that is almost fit to watch. My problem was almost solved when my smaller half snatched the switcher and punched a few buttons for herself.

After a dozen and two-thirds attempts, she settled on C-Span, the *educational* network. If you think that it isn't educational, you should sit and watch it for a couple of hours during a rousing session of Congress. Be sure to sit in a hard chair so that you will wake up in time to turn it off. C-Span is where I take most of my adult education classes in political science. One needs a class in analytical science to figure out what they are doing to earn all that money you are paying them.

I try to get my adult sex education time in by watching Andy Griffith in Mayberry and The Beverly Hillbillies. Other television programs dwell too long and too graphically on such things as violence, sex, violent sex, illicit sex, unnatural sex, sex and violence, animal violence, animal sex, plant sex, plant violence, and plant and animal sex and violence. The choice is varied, so take your pick.

And that is just on the news channels.

You may want to turn one of those on and sit and watch long enough to turn it off.

Don't worry if you tune in late. They are just like the old-timey movie theaters. They repeat every thirty minutes and you can go out right where you came in.

C-Span is different. I have been watching it for nigh on to five years now and I have seen less than a dozen characters on it who have tried sex. (Ed. note: That was before Clarence and Anita and Senator Bob). I'm not sure about their parents. Of course, most of that programming is live from the floor of the House and un-live from the floor of the Senate, or vice versa.

The program my little half finally landed on featured the president of The American Bar Association which should not be confused with that other bar group called "flies." I really wasn't paying much attention because he kept interrupting my train of thought while I was trying to read some worthwhile article in the latest edition of Hillbilly by some guy named Bill something or other. My readers know that my train of thought often travels without the caboose.

My ears are equipped with a unique detuning device. I haven't done any research among very many males of my species, having spent most of my available time researching the opposite, so it may be that I only think it is unique. It tunes out a lot of the noises I don't want to hear, like my bride telling me the lawn should be mowed this evening while it is nice and cool.

On our mountaintop last evening, it was hovering just a shade above eighty in the shade. That is only nine degrees older than me, so I pretended not to hear.

About an hour or so later as the time flies, I mentioned that I might start giving some serious thought to mowing the lawn in a day or two if the temperature dropped to a degree or so below my age.

It is a funny thing about wives and the amount of influence they wield. What it is is brute power. It is completely out of proportion to their size. I woke up this morning and discovered the lawn had been mowed and the driveway swept. It must have been done sometime after she made the eighth gentle suggestion. I have no idea who did it, but my back sure was sore when I tried to get out of bed.

It is a funny thing about my ears, too. When something pops up like the statement that guy made, the outsized flaps on the sides of my head increase to about three or four times normal size and trap everything in sight.

I think that what caught my divided attention and riveted it to one spot was the sounds in his voice. I could swear he was sobbing and trying to talk at the same time. He was definitely complaining about the utmost disrespect shown to attorneys, lawyers, shysters, barristers, and other associated beings in the political and judiciary fora.

He contended that writers, speakers, clients, ordinary citizens, and a few others should show some appreciation for what members of his organization have done for this country. I'm not at all sure that the preposition is correct.

Here in West Virginia, we are blessed with a plentitude of honest lawyers, but those of us who never progressed beyond a high school diploma and some of us who fell out before the sheep got skinned can't spell worth a hoot.

As a result of our lack of advanced education, we still spell attorney with a capital C, a little r, two little o's, and a k. When you put them all together they don't spell Mother, even if you feel like saying, "Mama Mia" sometimes.

I know that we have downright upright honest attorneys here, because I saw a shingle one time that read, "Honest Lawyer Upstairs, One Flight Up." His office was on the third floor. That should tell you something, even if only that he couldn't afford a new one and had bought the sign at a flea market.

I talked with a lady just yesterday who told me of a widow whose husband had been killed in an automobile accident. A Charleston lawyer heard the news on TV and hotfooted it to her house to talk her into letting him make her a fortune through the contingent-fee process which has become so popular. It has now spread to one or two other states.

Every Charleston lawyer that I have ever met took pride in his honesty, whether he was already deep in state government or just watching from the sidelines.

He did win the case and received a tidy sum in settlement. His share of the take and the few additional unexpected expenses took her share plus a few thousand

8

that she and her husband had managed to squirrel away against a snowy day.

That lawyer enjoys his income thoroughly and lives by the old adage, "Easy come, easy go." Some guy named John wound up with a good chunk of the widow's mite. I heard that John has changed his name, but it used to be Barleycorn.

That incident may or may not be true. It is close enough to the truth to sound like truth. Cases such as that can in no way be considered isolated. Ask any group of heirs which has been involved in estate litigation. Ask any attorney who is honest enough to give you an honest answer. There are some.

If that president of the ABA wants his members to have the respect of every Tom, Dick, and Mary in this country, he should start by slapping his proteges with a two-by-four in a rather sensitive spot to get their attention. He should then insist they practice what he preaches in order to earn that respect.

I believe that honest lawyers are in the majority. Outside of government, that is. There are some who have given the profession a bad name. They need to do some deep-cleaning on their red carpets.

An Open Letter to Walt Thayer

Author's note: Walt lives in Wenatchee, WA. He responded to an article which I had written about some of the unordinary foods we used to eat when I was a boy on the farm. I mentioned delicacies like groundhog, poke sallet, raccoon, grouse, pig tails and ears, souse, and one or two other gourmet treats. Walt wanted to know if I had ever eaten a few delicacies which he named. One of those was Walt's house specialty, some kind of oyster which grows on hillsides and on certain juveniles of a particular four-legged species. I hadn't.

It was just after my cataract surgery, so Walt had to wait an extra day or two to get his answer.

Dear Walt:

I wanted to reply to your letter sooner, but I couldn't tell an oyster from a dilberry while that doctor had his finger stuck in my eye.

We called ours "mountain oysters," Walt, since we were several yards east of the rockies and all of our sheep were the tame variety so we didn't have to run as fast to pluck a few of the dainty morsels. Most of us older hillbillies carried a sharp hawkbill to aid in plucking. I was too young at the time to be allowed to carry a knife, not even a dull one.

I always left them for the others who thought they needed them. They were supposed to be a good antidote for your procrastinating about your housework.

10

I'm pushing seventy-two and I'm still leaving them. They rank right down there with baked buzzard breast, crow cordon bleu, sauteed skunk, puree of 'possum, and barbecued copperhead ribs on my list of delicious foods. We had already eaten all the rattlesnakes in that part of the country long before I was born.

I did learn about your Angels on Horseback somewhere back there in time. I have nibbled on a few of those. They were made with real Chesapeake Bay oyrsters (correct pronunciation) drudged off the bottom near Point Lookout and Bloody Point Light. That was back there before they started drinking all that stuff that floats down the Potomac and the Susquehanna. I don't bother them any more. I figure if they can survive that, they deserve a second chance. I might even deserve that many myself. I haven't given up entirely on the bacon yet, but that may be because of my remote location in relationship to the pigsty.

But I can reccomember when a nice big Bay oyster snagged on a trolled Tony spoon and opened right over the side of the boat and sprinkled with a little salt and more black pepper and slurped down before all the bay water had drained from it was something to write home about and then drool over for days to come.

I never tried to pilfer one from some Oyrster-man's private stock. Some of those guys slept with one eye open and the 1903-06 loaded. No bluepoint was worth an even trade for a softpoint, especially one that might collide with some prominent spot.

We did eat some exotic foods that most modern sophisticated people haven't tried recently. We ate groundhogs, just like most every other bunch of hillbillies who couldn't afford to kill a good laying hen until she started lying. Groundhogs were good if they were cleaned and cooked properly. That opinion may have been strongly influenced by the empty-stomach syndrome.

We hunted 'coons for the pelts, but no coon carcass ever went to the dogs or the trash until the bones had been picked clean. They were as good as groundhogs.

I never saw a wild bear until I was tall-growed. Somebody must have beaten us to them. I'll guarantee you that we would have eaten one if it had stood still long enough for us to sink our teeth in him somewhere close to his hindquarters.

The deer were long gone from that area by the time I came along. They came back after a bunch of those awful animal killers, the hunters, came along with their ideas of propogation and conservation. I can't remember a single "animal rights" group or individual that kicked in any support for the restocking.

The deer have just about run the locals out of farm and barn because of all the efforts of the hunters. There are enough bears to kill off a few of the fawns.

We ate wild greens as soon as they were unsmart enough to punch their heads through the topsoil to get a taste of fresh sunshine. Dandelion greens, poke sallet, wild cress, broadleaf plantain, wild lettuce, and a dozen or so others and soaked our homemade breadcrusts in the pot likker to fill our bellies. I didn't learn to sample ramps until a few years later, but I have since made up for the shortfall.

And by the way, Walt, in case you don't remember what a dilberry is, those are the little black things we made tea over and used it to bring out a reluctant case of measles. We found them by following a likely-looking sheep. I'm glad that my measles were the early-popping kind. I don't think I could have handled the cure.

Well, Walt, it's been nice talking with you. I've got to get back to my word processor before it forgets what it is supposed to be doing. Hope this brings back some pleasant mountain memories.

Let me hear from you when you get a chance.

Your old pal,
Bill

Have you ever noticed that most males of the species seem to have more room in their hip pockets to stuff stuff like road maps, empty wallets, bandannas, knives, etc. than do their female counterparts?

My Recent Operations, Part One

All of us older folks have one thing in common. We have a noticeable tendency to talk too long in one place. Most of us like to talk about ourselves.

One of our favorite topics of conversation is our declining health. The prevalence of this apparent abnormality has caused me to assign a name to it. I call it the "Berdine Syndrome." I call other things by the same title, so be careful you don't become confused by similar-sounding names for different maladies. They all have a common ancestor.

I call it that because I am one of its carriers. I'm not sure if it is a contagious disease like the one that Typhoid Mary toted into this country and passed around among her friends and their acquaintances. I do know that it is almost universal among older people, particularly those who have just passed thirty and are feeling the effects. There are a few other major or minor requirements which seem to come automatically with aging.

I have studied The Berdine Syndrome for several years now with only a few interruptions. I have not reached any conclusion that you could clamp your dentures on as the cause, but I have reached the point where I can at least recognize some of the symptoms.

I do have some idea that the condition has been aggravated, if not actually induced, by the recent and not-so-recent appearances on television commercials of

14

some of the very ailments that we have come to enjoy so much when we talk about them.

I have noticed a dramatic increase in the number of such ads since I retired a little more than eight years ago. I have seen some of them so many times that I am beginning to have some of those same symptoms. The ailment seems to strike swiftly, usually within minutes after the resumption of that necessary evil in telecasting, the regular programming.

I suppose you have seen some of the same things I have, since most of them seem to air right before, during, or just after meal time when you can't help but watch and be fascinated by some pretty girl who has exactly the same symptoms you do and who can describe them so eloquently. I have been sorely tempted to use some of the same words and phrases to describe my afflictions.

I tried to get a chance to use them the other day, but I made a mistake in choosing my partner. She used the words before I could get my dentures unstuck from the glue powder that had overflowed and fastened top and lower hopelessly together, albeit temporarily.

Take P.M.S. for example. I have never suffered from that malady, but I have known people who did. Thinking back, I seem to recall that most of the elderly that I have heard talking about it were mostly female. I think. The older one of those gets, the worse it was.

I can't remember the name of the medicine recommended for the treatment of that ailment.

There was a young lady on TV telling me what to do in case I contracted it. She popped the name of the medication on me just as I popped two or three slices of raw cucumber into my mouth and I missed what she said. I wish I had listened more carefully. It sounded like something I might want to introduce into the conversation when it starts to lag.

Another commercial came on just as my wife set a big plate of country-fried steak, mashed potatoes and gravy, whole kernel corn, broccoli with horseradish sauce, two fresh hot rolls, a bowl of salad, and a big dish of applesauce in front of me. That was for lunch.

That commercial told how to stop diarrhea in its tracks, so to speak. I just missed the name, but I did hear the lady say that it wasn't (or maybe was) that pink stuff. My wife has a decided knack for interrupting something important when I am listening so intently. I can hardly wait for lunch time tomorrow so I can hear it again.

That commercial was followed almost immediately by another that told me what to do in case the big bowl of applesauce failed to perform its ordinary function properly and in case I couldn't get a good case of diarrhea just when I needed it most.

The lady who was trying to tell me the name of the remedy was keeping me in suspense. I became so eager to hear the name that I started inching forward in my chair. I reached the very edge and upset a steaming cup of coffee into my lap. I missed the name again.

16

There is another ad which comes on for a remedy for the same discomfortable feeling. It comes on long after the other one airs. It features a few wild animals that are obviously suffering from some of the same problems which affect so many of us older humans. When that owl gives out with his half-hearted hoot, I know exactly how he feels. He probably ate too many skinny mice for supper last night, bones and all.

That is the only product name I can remember. I may recall that one because I haven't been interrupted by something so unimportant like food and sustenance. I do need an occasional mental nudge from my wife.

I'll swan, that woman never forgets anything like that. There are two or three things from fifty or more years back that I wish she would forget. Those were the times when I made some SigmundFreudian or AlfredKinseyan slip which won't slip her mind.

If I do get non-diarrhea, that is the medicine that I will likely buy when the applesauce fails. Unless they start making me forget its name by showing the commercial drama at suppertime.

The only other commercial of any importance which is normally served with dinner is for some sort of device some female claims is the successor to something some man invented several years back and which any woman with half-ingenuity could have designed better and did. I missed the name of that one too. I have been watching the commercial carefully to see if they will exhibit it in person so I can duplicate it in my workshop.

17

I am considering whittling one out of a used crosstie and inserting it between the spaces on the video tape. I would have done it already, but I learned that they have an inexhaustible supply of reasonable facsimiles of those tapes.

I will never understand why the stations hold all the Ford commercials until after I have finished eating. They probably don't want to turn my stomach.

Author's historical note: They have now started doing that--after they learned just how bad the boys and Fords and Chevvies really were. It's enough to make you want to buy an import.

One of the most common greetings down here on top of this mountain is "How d' ye?" among some friends and acquaintances who haven't seen you in a while. We have shortened it to "Howdy," but most of us older youngsters know what it really means. If you ask us, we'll tell you. Some of us will tell you before you get a chance to say anything.

Any of the above greetings (and/or others) will give us an open door to a protracted propaedeutic conversation about the same subjects covered so inadequately by the ladies in the television commercials.

Come to think of it, I can't recall seeing a man doing the ads. Maybe we men should form an organization of our own. We could call it COSE, pronounced "cozy." The letters stand for Congress Of Sexual Equality. Membership would be limited to full-fledged males. And we would refuse to do the plug plug.

18

When I can locate someone who will listen, I try to place my one or two cohorts on either side and work the talkee into a corner, so that he can't slip by my assistants. I try to choose my audience very carefully, but sometimes you just have to make do with whatever you can get. I don't like to run into a person who is in worse shape than I am, especially if he wants to talk about his ills.

Some of those people get started on their own ailments before you can say, "Howdy." It is nigh on to impossible to get into the conversation except with your red ear. Some people even give you a blow-by-blow account of their trips to the john.

I'm not like that. I hardly ever discuss my bodily functions with strangers, unless they show some proclivity for listening to such details.

I do want to tell you about my operations, but that will have to wait until next time. My favorite television commercials are just starting and my wife is ready to serve supper. I'll tell you next time I see you.

My Recent Operations, Part Two

All of us who fall under the category of senior citizens have a common failing. We talk to anyone who is foolish enough to listen. Our favorite topics are ourselves, our poor health, and our operations.

Some of us get carried away with our own importance at times and tend to believe that everyone else is interested in our physical problems, especially those people in our age group which encompasses everything from slightly under twenty-nine to a few years past one hundred.

I have been surveying the group since I joined it recently although I was much too young. I have observed that the average age of seniors seems to be declining. Complicated calculations indicate that increasing numbers of people are becoming old at twenty-five or so and throwing the equation out of kilter. It may be that the late-twenties group is just now beginning to recognize the value of ill health as a conversational asset.

Many of us can talk at length on any subject. Those subjects may once in a great while include politics and religion, but we try to steer clear of controversial issues. Those two have become real hot potatoes in recent months, particularly the abortion and AIDS discussions which involve a good deal of both politics and religion. We may not have the foggiest notion of the real problems, but we are willing to give them our best lips.

If any of us has had an operation at any time in our long lifetime, we need to tell someone about it. Almost everyone past the age of seventy has had at least one. Some of us have been luckier than others and have enjoyed three or four. We may find it necessary to tell some person as many as four or five times in order to make him understand that our misfortune-turned-opportunity was a wee bit worse than anyone else ever experienced.

I have never had to repeat the operational history myself, but I know one person who tells about hers at least three times without stopping to catch her breath.

I certainly don't want to bore you with my operations, but it is almost impossible to use examples to illustrate the problem without mentioning somebody's. They might as well be mine.

The operations we like to talk about may be something as simple as that time about forty years ago when I had a cyst the size of a pea removed from my leg without benefit of anaesthesia, not even local. It is much better if the surgery is more complicated.

While I am already on the subject, let me tell you a funny thing or two about that cyst. It was located right at the point where my Bean boots slopped back and forth against my leg. I think the problem occurred because my shanks are so skinny that there wasn't enough bone and meat to fill the top of the lace-up boot, even when the sides were overlapped. I've had the slack-shank problem all my borned days.

21

The cyst just kept getting bigger. I soon realized that it had become a real conversation piece. I sat around in church and poolrooms with my good pants pulled halfway to my knee so that it couldn't help be noticed by anyone peering at my underpinnings. I could tell my grandchildren about it and anyone else's grandchildren who would be polite enough to not walk away while I was still talking. I did notice a few people duck into another aisle in the grocery store when they spotted me in the other end.

I finally listened to my wife's nagging and took my cyst to Dr. Coogle, leg and all. I hated to lose it. It was becoming so attached to me.

The first piece of gear that he shucked from the glass case was a hypodermic needle. It wasn't one of those teeny things like you see today. When I lived on the farm, we used a trocar on horses and cows that had sneaked into the green corn and become bloated. The trocar was the size of a long lead pencil and had a tube attached. The tube was nearly as big as one of those old-timey tire pumps. The tool Doc had in his hand made the trocar look like one of its runty offspring.

I could remember the loud hissing sound of gas escaping under extreme pressure when the trocar was stuck between the ribs of a bloated cow. I could picture my legs becoming skinnier. I was afraid it might drain something important from somewhere higher up. I didn't dare lose any more of that. Particularly that gray stuff just under my hair follicles.

I said to him, "Law, John, you surely don't intend to stick me with that thing." He came right back, just as sharp as could be, "Bill, that's to numb the area so I can cut without hurting you."

I took another look at the blunt end of that big long stick-um-a-jig and popped up, "Let me feel the edge of your whittlin' knife." You see, I was an old-timey meat cutter and I had been sliced a few times with a sharp knife. And that one was keen, let me tell you.

After I tested the edge with my thumb, I told him to forget the needle and just go ahead and cut away.

He protested, but he made four or six quick slashes and pitched a marble-sized chunk of shank meat on the table. I never flinched, although the hole was almost the size of a golf ball.

He made a couple of passes with his butcher knife at the ball of fat. What do you think was in that thing?

It was a big old hair, coiled up just as cozy as you please. He grabbed the end with a pair of tweezers and kept pulling until he stretched that hair out to all of twelve inches.

The boot had damaged the follicle so that it couldn't get its head out. It just kept growing and coiling like a fifteen inch snake.

My wife thought all the time that I had been putting her on by talking about the odd growth on my leg. I asked John if I could take it home to show her. He said he had to send the meat off to the packing house, but I could keep the hair.

When I pulled that eighteen inch hair out of my wallet to show her, she like to fell over.

That surgery is old hat now, but once in a while somebody will corner me and cajole and whine and won't let me loose until I tell them about the softball-size cyst with the twenty-one inch hair inside. It has been so long since I told the story that the thing may have grown another six or eight inches by now.

My next operation came just in time to provide a new story to replace the one which had grown kind of stale. I was beginning to forget some of the details without some kind of prompting from my wife.

It was about thirty years later. It was the fall after I retired nine years ago and I was becoming desperate for a new conversation piece.

I was at the farm in Upshur County in mid-August. The farm is a little bit of sidlin' ground that was left in my wife's family from the original tract settled by her ancestors when that country was unplowed ground.

I had been working like a real farmer, mowing high grass and cutting filth, trying to keep the lower four in decent shape. All other farms have a lower forty, but that one doesn't have enough lower to call it that without lying more than I'm used to.

You hardly ever hear of farmers cutting filth any more. They do the same thing except for the big difference in equipment. The muscles today are bigger and the endurance time is considerably longer. Farmers now call it brush hogging.

Brush hogging is done with a heavy-duty rotary cutter attached to the power take-off of a farm tractor. The tractor furnishes the manpower. The hardest work in brush hogging today is in steering the tractor and fixing flats that happen when you are paying more attention to the hired girl than to your steering. Most farmers I have known weren't exactly blessed with a one-track-ter mind.

Cutting filth the way we did it is accomplished by a body that can be either able or unable, depending upon which kind and size of bib overalls it is wearing. Mine were faded blue denim. With twisted suspenders.

The body furnishes the tractor power for any one or more of a variety of tools which the arms on the body may be wielding at any given time. These tools may include, but not be limited to, an axe, a mattock, a grubbing hoe, a Swedish axe, a Swedish buck saw, an Austrian scythe, (and you thought only some other nationality did stuff like that), a brush scythe attached to a crooked snathe, or some other equally cumbersome tool that doesn't require a lot of intelligence to operate improperly. Those fit my category and come nearer to being within the price range of my hip-pocket banker.

I had been operating several of those in the hot morning sun and the sweat was pouring. I kept looking toward the house to see if my wife was still there. When she yelled for me to come to lunch, I dropped whatever tool I was plying and took off at a dead run for the country kitchen.

25

I finished lunch and decided to relax and cool down a bit before returning to my delightful pastime. I just happened to glance down at my left hand. "Lookie there, Margy. There's a hole in the back of my hand."

I skedaddled out of there the next morning and headed for my young country doctor. By the time I went into surgery three weeks and three doctors later, there was nothing but some loose skin holding my thumb to the rest of my hand.

The crazy bone had been affected. The one in my arm. The nerve had grown fast to the bone and was on its last legs. I got it stopped in the nick of time. The doctor said it hadn't spread to my head, but there has since been considerable debate.

I had just about worn out my shrinking circle of friends with that topic of conversation when along came the last one and gave me a new lease on gassing.

I was fortunate enough to go into Princeton Community Hospital this past Monday for cataract surgery. I should have something to talk about for the next ten or twelve years.

The contingent fee lawyers and their willing accomplices who want to hit the jackpot for some real or imagined injury have driven medical costs out of sight. They have forced doctors to perform tests to protect their fortunes and reputations and other parts of their anatomies. I had been checked by four ophthalmologists before I got to the one who was to do the operation. I was checked by three other doctors and

26

I don't know how many nurses afterward and before they would let me into the hospital.

I could understand getting blood work, urinalysis, chest x-rays, an EKG, and a general physical. I'll be hanged if I can understand how I got mixed up with a podiatrist who said I had a malformed toenail. I often get confused, so I may have wandered into her office by mistake. She wouldn't let me out the door until she had given me a thorough going-over. I don't understand why I had to take off my pants so she could see my feet.

The doctors found me to be just a little more than perfect. I don't know the total cost of that, but my wife could have told them that. She has been saying that for nearly four years now. I can't remember what she said during the other forty-nine.

When I went directly from the last doctor to the hospital, the nurse handed me a plastic cup and pointed to the little room across the hall. I tried to explain to her that I didn't think I could because I just had. When they wanted to take more blood, I told them that I couldn't spare any more. I had just given at the office.

The nurse snatched the little cup and her accurate-puncture needle and shoved them back into the cabinet.

One of the nurses escorted me to a corner room with a flimsy curtain for a door. The curtain lacked about a foot-and-a-half of reaching the floor and either side. She handed me a gown and said, "Take everything off and put this on. Tie the blue strings together, then tie the white ones together."

I asked, "Everything?" "Yes, everything." There wasn't enough robe to cover my six-three long and two-twenty-five wide shame all over the front, let alone behind, and the back was split all the way up. Wide!

I tried to hide behind the narrow door of the locker, but a few ill-suppressed giggles told me that I was not entirely successful. I finally got the strings tied behind my neck, but I may have broken her first rule.

She handed me a pair of child's socks and told me to put them on my size eleven feet. She watched. When I finally stretched them as far as my heels, she said to a second nurse who had come to watch, "Uh, oh. He should have had blue booties."

I'm not sure if she was referring to sock size or to the abrupt disclosure when I gave them that last tug. I was not born a Scotsman, so I know nothing about how one should put on his socks while wearing a split kilt.

I did learn one thing. I now know that some things may blow hot and cold, but hospital air conditioners aren't one of them.

She told me to get into bed. Three more nurses had appeared by that time to observe my discomfiture. I'll guarantee you that I had lots of it. They all stood by to watch. I did. The bed was only sixty-eight inches long and both feet dangled over the end. The sheets were even shorter. I borrowed a coat from the next-door lady patient whose visit had turned into a holiday. I needed it to cover my shame when the sheets and robe started their inevitable upward mobility.

It wouldn't have been so bad if eight different nurses hadn't found some excuse to walk past my bed and peek in to see if I was all right. They didn't have to snicker every time they passed.

One especially pretty nurse came in alone and said that she was Miss Mean. She took one quick glance and said, "Good grief." She took off down the hall with both hands covering her face and chuckling every step. I have no idea what caused her change in attitude. She seemed happy enough when she left.

The performance was repeated when I was wheeled into pre-op but the cast was new. I got so embarassed that I forgot which eye was to undergo surgery.

I went into surgery and wouldn't you know that my luck ran true to form. Some bloomin' salesman came in while Doc was chopping at my eye and tried to sell him a vacuum cleaner or something. All the time I was on the table. I hope he lost the sale.

I did hear the nurses chatting in the hall when I came back. They were still giggling. I heard one of them say, "That is the guy who wrote that hilarious book." Maybe that's what they were laughing at. But only four of them asked for my autograph.

I haven't had time to think up a funny story for that operation. As soon as I come up with one, I'll let you know. You may just want to read it in the paper.

Some Funny Stuff that Went on Right Under My Nose

I have a years-ago friend who retired and moved to Florida some time back. His Hillbilly Highway wasn't leading to work, just his place in the sun.

I saw him once after he had been living in the Bikini State a short while. My first remark to him was, "Tom! I figured that when I saw you, the soles of your feet and your eyeballs would both be sunburned." "Oh, My Land, Bill, they were. You can lay down there on the beach and see some sights that will make you roll your cigarettes so tight you can't draw through them."

That same friend lived on the banks of the Guyandotte River, a slow-flowing warm-water stream which drains the watershed inhabited by several miners and the mines which supported them.

Tom had been looking at chain saws for a few weeks, trying to determine which would be best for his few projects. His wife beat him to the punch when she bought him a new Mac for his birthday.

Tom couldn't wait to use it. He already knew how, being a miner by trade and a mine superintendent by something more than accident.

He filled it with fuel mixture and cranked it up. It started as all good chain saws should. He shut it off, tied a line to the handle and climbed a riverside tree. The tree had an unsightly limb which stuck out over the river and which had eaten several of Tom's lures.

He pulled the chain saw up beside him where he sat

on the offending limb. He fired up the saw and proceeded to get even with it.

The noise of the saw must have drowned out his wife's shouts. When the saw made its way through the limb, the saw, Tom, and the limb landed in the river. That was the last time he sat on the outboard end of a limb while he sawed it off near the trunk.

Tom ran one of the mines on my list of calls. That was 'way back there in that other life of mine when someone told me that I was a salesman. It was just before I learned to spell it and long before I never really became one.

I had come home with stories about Tom and his personal life. They were all told to me by him and one or more may have been true. I have a whole pocketful of "Tom" tales which will never pass my word processor and which I will never tell my wife. They fly in the face of ethical newspapering, but I might write a book some day. That is my own opinion, of course. A few of them might make the scandal sheets without raising a single eyebrow.

My wife often traveled with me on some of my short trips and on nearly all of my long ones. I suspected that she suspected that some other wily female might suspect that I was fair game and try to trap me, although by that time I had become sort of bait-shy. Especially if the bait started chasing me. I decided that it might be safe to let her meet Tom after I had told him not to tell too much of everything he knew.

I surprised him in his office one day by telling him that I had someone outside who had been listening to some of my stories. I wanted him to meet her--or more precisely, I wanted her to see the guy who was the hero of all those stories.

Tom was totally devoid of permanent dentures except for the portable kind. He normally carried his uppers and lowers in a pocket of his mine clothes to keep them from getting dirty.

When I made my announcement, Tom began poking in all his pockets, one after the other, frantically searching for his wayward mouthpieces. I guessed what he was doing.

"For goodness sake, Tom, I just wanted you to meet her, not kiss her." He shot back, "They don't call me Killer for nothing."

I was underground at Tom's mine another time trying to jackknife my six-three and two-twenty-five frame into the under-forty inches of space between the top and bottom. The roof bolt heads kept clawing at the knobs on my spine, drawing blood and almost-dirty remarks at every other restricted step.

Some regular miner came tearing past me so fast that he was raising bug dust. When I went outside, I told Tom about the guy who was a sheer genius at negotiating the low coal at break-back speed.

Tom mentioned him by name and added that he wouldn't come past my belly-button when he stood straight up.

When the man trotted past me on the way to the bathhouse, I saw what Tom meant. He stood just barely higher than the pucker on my abdomen--with his hard hat on.

I nailed him. "You little rascal, you gave me what-for in there on the section, but I'll run you a footrace out here in the open."

He broke up. So did Tom.

This next story was told to me by an innocent by-stander who swore on his MSA lamp that it was true.

Tom had a trusted foreman on one of the sections. He became involved in a bit of fisticuffs with one of the union miners. Tom questioned him as soon as he came into the office in order to get a truthful report on the incident. Like all stories such as that, there were two sides. Tom heard the foreman's.

The V.P. had heard the story from someone else before Tom reached his office to make his report. When Tom told the veep that the union man had struck the first blow, he asked, "You wouldn't lie to me, would you Tom?" Tom popped back with as sober an expression as he had ever worn, "Mr. ----, I wouldn't lie to you unless I thought I needed to." The veep broke down.

I haven't seen Tom for several years now. The last time I heard through a mutual friend, he was still going out on his boat and catching a bass or a crappie every now and again. Maybe the sun didn't get to him yet.

How to Keep a Trout

Most of you who have read my column for any length of time and all of you who have read my book, "The Berdine Un-Theory of Evolution and Other Scientific Studies Including Hunting, Fishing, and Sex" know that I don't reveal many of my fishing secrets and even less of someone else's who is kind enough to share one or two with me.

I am especially particular about my favorite walleye holes and my secret lures. I never share those with anyone other than my wife. I have tried that a couple of times and wound up with less secrets than before.

I have a friend and reader who shared his secret bass lures with me just this past week. He swore me to secrecy with my right hand on a copy of my book. He can feel safe that no one will find out from me unless they have some powerful bifocals and watch me from a distance while I am trying to confuse a wily bass.

I am about to let you in on a secret which was given to me by my good friend, India Brown. She is another of those remarkable women who know how to fix a fine kettle of fish after she catches them by herownself.

She is a bona fide member in good standing of The Mercer Angler's Club, an association of devotees of the fine art of trout fishing. They have their own pond.

Don't get all fretful and upset. I asked her first if I could share it with the rest of my friends. Being the kindly person that she is, she gave her assent.

The first thing you need to do in order to properly preserve a piscatorial prize for future eating is to catch one. If they are running on the runty side, you may want to catch three or four. Sometimes there is a big gap between want-tos and can-dos.

If you are one of those fishermen who want to but can't, you could strike up a friendly conversation with a fellow who has been making you jealous. This activity requires extreme tact and the proper amount of servility if you want to wind up with a few fish. If you overdo any phase of it, the approachee may tell you to go get your head wet.

I have interviewed hundreds of trout fishermen in my lifetime. Most don't seem to mind for anyone to keep a few fish as long as you don't overdo it. Unless it is another fisherman who is catching and keeping while they are standing there looking hungry.

Game wardens sometimes wear garb to make them look like a wolf in fisherman's clothing. It's best not to pick on one of them if you decide to try to bum a few.

I have interviewed thousands of trout that I have caught and they don't seem to object too much to being kept. Unless you count the fighting and wiggling they do to get off the hook. To be absolutely honest with you, I have kept a precious few to eat. I would bet that I haven't killed more than two dozen trout for my own use in the more than fifty years I have been fishing for them. 'Way more than fifty. I have taken a few for fishermen who were more hungry than fortunate.

I wouldn't think of trying to tell you where to fish or what bait to use. You probably know all of that already or you wouldn't be reading this. We do have one or two fair-to-middlin' trout streams here in West Virginia. I learned that from reading one of those outdoor magazines. I have fished another hundred or so they didn't mention. I won't either.

If you stumble upon a trout stream by chance or go there by intent, you may or may not catch trout. They are funny that way. If you can't land a trout, don't fret. The recipe works just as well for crappie, catfish, blue-gills, bass, or pike. I wouldn't swear about carp.

Skin your catch or filet it. I prefer to filet mine, but the only fish I ever keep to eat is that strange-looking specimen with the glassy eyes.

My favorite method for skinning a trout of medium size is to make a crosswise cut just behind the head and not quite all the way through. Split the skin on both sides of the dorsal fin and all the way back to the tail. Peel the skin at the cross cut back on both sides until you have a triangle of flesh exposed that is about an inch or two long and most of the way down toward the belly. Insert a forefinger into the cut and hold tight. Grasp the head and break it sharply downward. Be sure the skin starts to peel as you continue to pull downward and away from the body. The trout should come out like peeling a banana.

Pack the pieces loosely in a freezer container. The size will depend upon how lucky you were.

Cover the pieces with clear cold water. Squeeze two drops of juice from your favorite lemon or reasonable facsimile into the water. Add one-half teaspoon vinegar to the quart of water and don't heap the measure. Dash quickly one dash of salt from the salt-dasher and don't over-dash. Put the lid on firmly and store in the freezer. When you feel like a fine fixin' of fish, remove and allow to thaw. Remove the water, drip dry on a triple thickness of paper towel. Unused ones seem to do much better. Pop the pieces into the pan and then into your oral cavity.

Don't try to fry the water. Water with lemon, salt, and vinegar added won't fry worth a hoot.

I take offense at the statement that fishermen are all liars. I never lie about my fishing trips nor the size of the ones I kept nor the ones that got away. My mind is like a lot of other guys', so I may not remember quite as clearly as I should, but I don't lie.

Is That Art? Art Who?

I've been on an art kick for two or three days now, having seen some real art and also having seen some ---.

The "some" was called art by people who buy art and claim they know what art art and what art not.

I sort of lost faith in art critics when one well-known critic picked up a piece of wood and said, "Now that is a beautiful piece of pottery." I could tell it was wood because I looked at the bottom. A distant acquaintance had carved his initials there and I knew he wouldn't want to get any clay under his fingernails.

I'll be hanged if I can understand why anyone would hang some of the "some" in his sparkin' parlor or in his boudoir unless he needed something to cover the hole in the dry-wall that suddenly appeared when he missed his girlfriend with his fist. If he bought it for that purpose, he should turn the painted side to the wall and hang a bunch of posies on the backside for the visitors to see.

There are several schools of painting, especially in those pictures (?) called art. Among those are such definitive names as Pop-art, Op-art, Art-deco, and three or four I haven't heard yet. I'm not much of an art critic, if you can put any stock in what the critics critique, but I certainly can and do criticize a lot of it.

The one with which I am most familiar, other than Mail Pouch Barn-art, seems to be conventional paintings, sometimes called Realistic art or, more commonly, "The School of Realism."

I saw one exceptional mural at one of our modern public facilities the other day that I thought was really well-done. It reminded me of some place I had been or seen, maybe both. It turned out to be a photograph taken by one of our good old West Virginia boys about six country miles from our house. I learned that by asking the kind of question for which I am famous.

It must have been run through the enlarger.

I have seen (on TV, of course) a passel of people stand in front of an incomprehensible painting and stare to their eyes' content. All the people in that group of forty or so well-dressed dowagers and dowage-hes were going "Oohh!" and "Aahh!" one right after the other and some of them at the same time.

I don't know which sound was coming from the hers nor which from the hes, but the "Aahhs" sounded a lot like the first part of a sound I make after my two-foot birdie putt rings the cup and bounces back to the grass.

I'll bet no more than one of the group had any idea about the conglomeration of smeared paint at which they were looking. I doubt that the artist had any idea about the message unless it was, "Don't kick your bucket while the canvas is still on the floor."

Unless, of course, you have a good press agent who could sell cowtracks full of water to flood victims.

Some of the other paintings I have seen--mostly on TV--didn't look like much of anything. I have my own nomenclature for that genre. I call it "Goof-art." It looked like the artist had already kicked his own.

I just watched a movie about a girl who became a rich widow by marrying a succession of poor boys who were on the verge of becoming financial successes. Just before they kicked their buckets.

One of those was an artist who became an overnight sensation when his pet monkey drug its tail across the paint tray and then over the few paintings which were lying around unsold and unwanted.

He went into mass production, using artificial tails made from bits of hair from horses, cows, and his bride's pony tail.

Texture is everything in painting. They sold like hotcakes at crepes-suzette prices. Just like in real life.

If I thought I could make money hand over elbow like he did, I'd run down to Lowe's and buy a box of brushes and three or four gallons of paint. Then I would get me three or four monkeys with long tails and put them to work at minimum wage.

It ought to be as good as some I've seen.

I could call it "Goof-art."

I have the mentality for it.

Now Ain't That a Fine Kettle of Fish (or How to Make Money Not Fishing)

If you are one of my regular readers, I know that you aren't going to believe this, but it was my wife who was watching NBC News on WVVA-TV this time. I was busy in another room thinking of something to write so Sandy wouldn't have to fill the newspaper with blank pages.

NBC News is another of my institutions of higher learning, but it usually isn't nearly as funny as some of the other news channels and C-Span.

I overheard that young fellow who does practically all the talking on that program say something that made me sit bolt upright. Sometimes I don't hear too well, but I could almost swear that I heard him say that The United States and Canada had shaken hands to an agreement to close the haddock patches off the east coast to all commercial fishing. That action left several big fishing boats all dieseled up and no place to go.

The commercial fishermen, all of whom had invested all their spare cash in hooks, lines, and sinkers, had turned man's favorite sport into a self-supporting hobby.

It seems, to hear the government tell the big fish story, that those fishermen just didn't know when to stop. They now want the government to start paying them for not catching fish. What a novel idea! I know how they feel.

The big fishing hole was closed because there were too few of those fine finny fellows who turn into French-fried fish filet finger food after they come ashore.

I can't say that I blame the fishermen for crying "Subsidy" the first time they get a little saltwater in their Shakespeares. We have given subsidies to just about everybody else and his mother, including farmers.

Those subsidies have included paying farmers for not growing corn, wheat, barley, potatoes, and cows.

We have at one time or another in my foggy memory painted potatoes blue and bought the speckled spuds by the ton and buried them so the hungry people couldn't snitch a few to keep their backbones from rubbing holes in their bellies. We still support peanut farmers so they can become millionaires overnight without doing any work. If you don't get a subsidy, you can't peddle your peanuts for love nor lucre.

We still regulate and support tobacco growers. Those programs have bankrolled over the years into billions of dollars.

There is one thing wrong with those programs. They rarely help the little guy, but they make the huge combines even richer.

We still support sleazy art and artists, although there is some indication that peer pressure properly applied is likely to curtail that to some extent. We might as well give fishermen at least enough to scrape the barnacles off their bottoms while they are laid up in port. They have been supporting the others for years.

Many of my readers know that I have caught fish, maybe more than my fair share. All but a few of those were turned back to furnish food and fun for others. I realize that is a bit different from poaching for fun and profit.

I have invested thousands of dollars over the past sixty-odd years in tackle, rods, reels, boats, motors, gasoline, bait, rentals, and all the other essentials. And those were the things for my wife. I have not shown a profit in any of those many years.

I can remember when I caught walleyes as fast as I could release one and get my line back in the water. Two minutes without a fish was considered slow fishing.

It isn't that way today. My wife logs our catches accurately. We went out in a blinding May snowstorm a couple of years back. I only caught sixty-eight in three hours.

I would like to know how to apply for some kind of government assistance to help offset my losses. I would be willing to accept a modest sum, say ten dollars per fish, for those I don't catch and double that for the ones I release to catch again. If I can keep my own tally.

Historical note: The governments are still holding out, but they are having some difficulty with out-of-state poachers. If they can stop alien fishermen, they may be able to salvage the cod, haddock, and halibut fishery yet.

Hale's Far

Now I want all you fellers to know that I was brung up on a farm. That farm was clean up in the head of the holler where the spring branch wasn't hardly big enough for a frog to get his britches wet. An' I want you all to know that when I was brung up fur enough to keep out from underfoot I was a-workin' in the hayfield. That was mostly in the summertime and when the sun was a-boilin' down jist as hot as she could get. We didn't put up no hay in no rainstorm.

I just wanted you to know that I wasn't always as sophisticated as my normal columns would lead you to believe.

I jist read t'other day about some feller who was complainin' about somebody a-settin' mought nigh a hunnert of his hay bales on far. I don't know where Mr. Hale lived, but if'n he lived around these parts, I'll bet he was a-usin' one o' them new-fangled balers that rolls the hay up in big round balls with the ends cut off kinder square. Them big ol' rascals will hold a heap o' hay--mought nigh as much as six or eight o' them little long square things that the haymakers started usin' at about the same time that I quit pilin' it around a tall skinny pole that we stuck in the ground for that very purpose. I ain't been up on no stack of hay since the last time I stuck a wisp of hay on the point for a bit of good luck. That has been more years than you can shake a pitchfork at.

One thing that I was tolt before I got the first chaff in my eyes, ears, nose, and throat and even down the inside o' my bib overhauls was that you don't put no green ner wet hay around no stackpole and then pile more on top of hit.

That lesson was brung home to me t'other day and jist before I read about Mr. Hale's far.

I looked out my kitchen winder at where some neighbor had been dumpin' his leftover grass clippin's behint one o' my tin sheds and I seen smoke a-comin' up out o' that pile. I went a-runnin' out there as fast as my seventy-two-year-old legs (they're the same age as me) would carry me to see if I could git her out before the whole shebang went up in smoke.

I jist figgered somebody had accidentally dropped his hot butt into the pile. It was jist a little ol' pile an' not hardly big enough to start its own far. It was too green to burn. But that warn't hit a-tall. What it was was what could have happened to Hale's hay, if'n he rolled her up a mite too tight an' a might too green.

I knocked the top off'n that pile an' don't you know that that there smoke was a-comin' up out o' the middle where nobody could've got his hot butt off his joint even if'n he had been a-tryin' to hide it from a peace officer.

I haff to prove everything to myself, sometimes twice, before I believe even what I see. I poked my forefinger down in that pile o' grass an' I can tell you right off that it didn't take me no two pokes to find out she was hot.

45

Now I ain't a-sayin' that Mr. Hale's far was caused by that there spontaneous combustion, mind you.

Maybe it was set by somebody with a hot butt to hide or by somebody who wasn't tryin' to evade persecution fer arson.

I jist want to tell all of you old farmers and all of you new ones that it jist don't pay to put yore hay up too green ner too wet.

Wait a couple o' days until she gits ripe.

Did you hear the one about the old-timey farmer who had two lovely daughters?

One day a handsome traveling salesman came by and the old farmer ordered a new buggy for each of them.

The salesman raced all the way back to the office to tell his sales manager about his biggest sale of the month.

You didn't expect him to telephone, did you?

The Initial Experiment

There could have been one or more reasons why this event missed its proper place in history. It was pretty much hush-hush at the time, especially by those directly involved, so it may have been withheld from the historians. They are a bunch of blabbermouths and the only secrets, top or bottom, they have been able to keep are those they never learned about until it was too late.

I do not know of one person who breathed a word of it outside the small group of participants and the limited circle of their closest friends, except where there was a need to know.

Before you begin to believe that I was one of the participants, I want you to know that I was merely one of the circle of friends. I wasn't told until the later stages and I have not revealed it until now.

It occurred at about the same time that there was some minor disquiet in Europe that had begun to sound as if the planet had a bad belly-ache that would soon erupt in a huge burp spelled w-a-r. Historians of the era and the available media representatives were all interested in what that moustachioed paper hanger was going to do next. If going to the moon had ever entered their minds, it was only as a Buck Rogers space fantasy.

I am writing the details now so that posterity will not be denied forever this bit of history that was of such importance to those who participated in it. I don't want this event relegated to the same position of unimportant

47

events of history that has been assigned to others such as the depredations on travelers in some of our counties, Lord Dunmore's War, the Cherokee raids and raideds, and a couple of others that either of us could name. The historians may learn of it now and still decide that it has no proper place in their books--but this one is mine.

I have spent considerable time in deliberation about whether or not it should even now be made public. I finally decided that disclosure would not seriously endanger national security as much as some of the information that The National Aeronautical and Space Administration (hereinafter referred to as NASA) has already released. If they can tell, so can I.

I have not, however, seen anything in the way of reliable data that would involve this research and the testing of the resultant theories. Knowing how many bigmouths there are in the bureaucracy and in the Congress who will tell everything they know or can find out for a few dollars slipped into their side pockets causes me to believe that the information may be stored in some ancient computer files marked "Documents For Public Viewing." They wouldn't think of divulging any information available to all and sundry.

It may have been erased by some bungler who had as many thumbs as I have. It would not likely be classified as "Top Secret, Eyes Only" any longer. It may never have been.

I always like to confuse my readers and make them think, so I am going to run true to form and start the story at the end and then lead you backwards through time and trials to the beginning. That was where it all started.

An astronaut by the name of Neil Armstrong was the first earthling, as far as we know from our limited history, to set foot on the moon. This momentous historical event was duly noted and well publicized at the time of the occurrence in newspapers, on the radio, and on television. It was one of the few things I have seen on television that I thought might possibly be believed. That may have been because there were no reporters willing to make the trip nor commentators to distort what we could clearly see with our own squinty eyes right there on the tube.

The date was July 20, 1969 as we reckon time. Our way may not be entirely accurate, but it is about as close as we have come in all of our millennia of trying to get it right. We may accomplish that at some time in the future, especially if we have a few more millennia to work on it. If we don't run out of time first.

One fact that most historians overlooked was that the landing occurred exactly one month after the 106th anniversary of West Virginia's secession from the union, The Confederate States of America.

Traveling non-stop to the moon and landing on it were only the culmination of many years of demanding and intensive research by space scientists. The walk and then the ride in that funny-looking little taxi were historical achievements for the space program. Neil deserved all the recognition and honors that he received when he returned and walked on that other not-quite-so-exciting bit of real estate in front of the NASA building in Houston. The other members of the crew were not so highly lauded, but they were every bit as deserving.

There is a long and complicated path that can be traced backward from that event that was the exclamation point at the end of the sentence. There were literally hundreds of other major scientific achievements along the way that were recorded as history at the time, but they faded into insignificance when they were compared to that landing and the planting of the American flag on the moon. Neil and the crew of the moon rocket ship allowed us to be the first to know that the moon was not made of green cheese.

"Green cheese" in the stories which had been handed down through countless generations over the centuries obviously referred to cheese that was not quite ripe, not to the color. Even us kids could see that. I'm not sure that our parents, grandparents, aunts, and uncles ever knew it, but we did.

The thousands of workers who conducted the research and testing along the way deserved some special recognition too. Their work had to be done, checked, rechecked and then tested and successful results obtained before Neil could change from his B.V.D.'s into his space suit.

There were remarkably few failures along the way. Some of those were particularly sad--enough to tear at your very soul and being. These, too, deserve their places in our history.

I have chosen to omit many of the details of that complicated process that led to the grand finale. My excuse is that disclosure might not be in the national interest. That is gobbledygook or doublespeak for "Ha, ha. You don't know either?" If only we could get our politicians and bureaucrats to be as honest and forthright. I have yet to hear but one of them answer any question with a simple "I don't know."

A lot of research and training must have gone into such a simple act as hitting that golf ball and driving it for two or three country miles. I have been playing golf for several years and have studied briefly under a number of pros. That translates into "They gave up after the first lesson." My drives rarely exceed a hundred yards. Other than distance, my drives are all just like that one--in the rough. It may be that I am holding the club by the wrong end.

I am not sure if those miles were earth miles and I don't know how those compare to moon miles. I do know how "Moon Pies" stack up against homemade apple, cherry or rhubarb pies. If pies are anything like miles, my drives may be every bit as long .

There was also that short jaunt in that doohickey of a thing that looked like a boxy garden cart with four wheels. Years of research and design must have gone into that thing. Even the tires were special. I saw it or a reasonable facsimile after they brought it back to Houston. It didn't look much like the 1936 Airflow Chrysler which was the most aerodynamically advanced car of its time and for many years after.

This chapter is made brief because I could not begin to list all of those who made significant contributions to the program. The American taxpayer and his progeny for several generations to come may not be the least of the bunch.

I would not want to slight anyone, not even the subject of our first propulsion experiment which was conducted in a place that shall also remain unamed. I wouldn't mention that person by name under any set of circumstances that I can imagine, although the experiment was carried out considerably more than fifty years ago. If he wants to admit it, that is up to him. But I don't want him to involve me.

As far as I know (and that may be less than half enough), some of my buddies conducted the first of such testing more than thirty years before Neil took his stroll. I am not mentioning any of them by name either. They must all be in their late seventies, but there may be one or two of them left with enough strength to operate the firing mechanism of a twelve gauge. Neither am I about to reveal the identity of the one who devised the ignition system. For reasons of national security. And because his father might still be living and would thrash the tar out of him for stealing his smokes.

I certainly don't want the enemy, whoever that is, to start looking for any of those giant scientific minds who invented the systems and carried out the experiments. If Hitler had ever found about us, he might have kidnapped the whole lot and won the war. And I never could learn to speak German.

The scientific value of the test we made cannot be adequately evaluated by the available criteria. That may be another reason why history ignored us. We were so far ahead of our time that the historians of that era could not comprehend what we were doing. As far as I know, NASA has not released any data on any other tests that were even remotely similar to ours.

Back there in those days when I was just beginning to get all my advanced education, some little bit of which was gained from hands-on experiences, there was a widely known and less widely administered spring medication known as Sulphur and Molasses.

I am always careful to give thanks for all my small blessings. One of those was that my mother did not give us that particular home remedy.

She was an intelligent woman, wise beyond her years and time. She had very likely heard of it. She had also more than likely had some contact with some of the aromas that always surrounded anyone who had been on the tonic for more than three or four days. That tonic, after three or four big doses, would start your sap to running. It also eliminated the need, albeit temporarily, of the regular draughts of mineral water.

Our mineral water was just plain old spring water in a pint canning jar that was filled just shy of the brim. The only thing that made it taste or act any different that I could determine was the heaping tea-spoonful of epsom salts that had been dumped into it and then thoroughly dissolved when you screwed the zinc lid down tight against the rubber and shook the container briskly.

That ingredient gave it a distinctive flavor and achieved one or two other minor results that ordinary old spring water wouldn't dare think about. It had a tendency to develop your leg muscles and your footwork so that you could do the hundred yard dash in your long johns with both hands behind your back on a cold morning in something under ten seconds flat. The reason that you ran with your hands behind was to avoid any waste of precious time at the last second.

And that was counting the time it took to loosen the frozen latch if you were the first in line. Those were the good old days you hear people talk about so much.

I have tasted some of that mineral water that retails for upwards of three dollars for a quart bottle with fancy pictures on it. That sampling has led me to believe that some sharp entrepreneur has access to a good supply of tap water and has pilfered our secret formula.

Water today just isn't the same kind of stuff that it was sixty or more years ago. You can take a drink from just about any lake or pond that was good water then and get the same results that we got then with the epsom salts. One good swig of lake water can easily make you irregular once or twice a week for as long as two or three years at a stretch.

Scientists have made some remarkable progress in the last few years. They have discovered a little bug so small you can't see it even when you are wearing your bifocals. It is called "giardia," but I'm not sure of the spelling. They have stuck them into just about every hole of good drinking water they could find in the U. S. and Canada. They may have sneaked a few into a couple of foreign countries as well.

The little rascals can multiply faster than rabbits. They go right on inside as well as outside. It doesn't help to boil the water after you drink it, but it does scald the feathers off the little rascals if you boil it first and drink it later--from another container. Boiling may scald off one or two other things as well. It slows down their reproduction.

The other thing that Sulphur and Molasses did was to advertise itself. It would cause you to stink to high heaven just standing around. It would also cause you to produce a high volume of gas and the process was just a mite more than continuous.

The gas smelled like the smoke directly off the fire and brimstone in that other place. I'm not spelling it out for you because of my years of close association with an older female relative who washed my mouth with lye soap every time I uttered one of those words in her presence. Enough of them sneaked out to cause me to have regular attacks of foaming at the mouth, but my teeth and gums were sterile. I have often wondered if Mom enjoyed that.

Some bright scientist in our Chemistry class (I'm not mentioning any names here either) got the idea that if the gas smelled like something that would explode or already had, it might burn readily, given the proper environment and conditions. He immediately decided to try an experiment, if he could find a reliable source.

That simple idea was all it took to start the wheels turning in several scientific brains. Not to mention diabolic.

One genius developed the ignition system. That was rather easy for him. He was the only one of the group that could afford to smoke anything besides rabbit tobacco. He had been snitching a little tobacco and a few papers from the packages of Bugler and Target that his father kept around the house.

He had been practicing for so long that he could roll a Camel with one hand and a Lucky with the other. Not at the same time, you understand.

The hand that was not manipulating the lumpy roll-your-own was busy grabbing a handful of farmer matches from the tin box that hung on the wall beside the wood-burning cook stove. And all that had to be accomplished while no one was watching.

The hardest part of the experiment turned out to be talking one of the freshman scientists into acting as the fuel source. We had already determined by some sixth or fifth sense that he was an able candidate.

He had been on the tonic for more than a week and the manufacturing process was in full swing. You could spot one of those producing well-heads even if he was around a corner and the breeze was right.

There were a few sore-heads around who claimed later that we had coerced him. It seems you always have a few of those second-guessers around just to make your life more difficult. My own opinion is that they were resentful because we didn't agree to open the experiment to observation by the general public or because they didn't think of it first.

There wasn't room in the space lab for everybody. And secrecy was the primary concern of the entire space program in the early years. Ours was no exception. We had to carefully screen every applicant.

I didn't know what "coerced" meant, but we didn't do any such thing. All we did was convince him that if he didn't go along with the program, we would incarcerate him in an isolated backhouse just before school started and block the door. We were only planning to leave him just the one day. That surely couldn't be construed as coercion.

That outside toilet sat atop a high hill and there was no running water, but there was usually a good breeze blowing almost every day in April. A day spent there in seclusion wouldn't have been too bad. After he rather half-heartedly agreed, we had to determine proper timing. NASA still does that, even with the space shuttle.

The football coach doubled as science teacher and assistant principal. A lot of people wore whatever hats didn't have other heads in them back in those days, so that multiple-use of one body was not unusual. Both he and the principal sort of frowned on extra-curricular experiments. Especially those that might lead to some remarkable discoveries.

That attitude may have been encouraged by circumstances. I clearly remember how upset they became when some ornery sophomore purloined a small piece of solid sodium from the storage container where it was submerged in oil to prevent accidental oxidation.

I feel sure that you know what happens when iron oxidizes. It rusts. You may not be quite so familiar with raw sodium. When it oxidizes, it doesn't act like iron. Not anything at all. It oxidizes rather quickly when exposed to air. The oxidation is so rapid you can see it with your naked eyes, which shouldn't be naked while conducting experiments with sodium. When the medium is water, the oxidation reaches highly accelerated speeds. It heats up to the ignition point of wood in about three seconds flat and the resulting uncontrolled explosion throws little pieces of fiery sodium hither, thither, and yon.

One of us was lucky enough to sit in as an observer during a controlled experiment demonstrating that remarkable characteristic. He filed the information in his hairy data bank for future reference.

That rotten kid took the pilfered chunk of sodium outside the basement door and chunked it into a can with about three inches of water in the bottom. Where else did you expect the water to be?

He was fast enough on his feet to be back inside the building and staring out the window when the sodium exploded and flew in all directions, leaving miniature jet trails as it went. And that was before there were any jet planes to leave trails in the clear blue yonder. But not by much.

The volunteer fire department arrived in less than four minutes (they may have had some advance alert) and extinguished the incipient conflagration by pulling two vertical boards from the corner of the school building. The piece of sodium that had taken refuge there and caused all the pinewood smoke was just a little old thing.

That experiment had absolutely no connection with our propulsion experiment except that the same budding genius was the dreamer and the thief. It did make us a bit leery of the coach and caused us to be concerned for the health of the principal cum History and Social Sciences teacher. The sodium experience had caused his face to turn a fiery red and his feet to make loud slapping noises as he stomped around the room, threatening and cajoling, trying to determine the identity of the culprit. If he ever did learn who it was, he never indicated it to me, and I would have known.

The coach developed a bad case of snickering behind

his handkerchief. He had a vivid imagination and could likely remember when he had been involved in some similar shenanigans. He was probably giving silent thanks that the school building was still standing, minus only two boards that could be nailed back in place some day when the weather was warmer.

When all signals were "A-OK" for the experiment to proceed, we headed for the basement lab. It is absolutely amazing that the timing coincided precisely with a time when the coach and the principal were involved in a meeting with an unruly student and another teacher or two and could not be disturbed.

Personally, I never did have much use for those kids who could never seem to obey the rules. They made life rough for those of us who did.

During the preliminary discussions that were hurriedly conducted as soon as we learned of the unexpected window of opportunity which had so conveniently presented itself, one brilliant mind remembered a side effect of spring tonic and mentioned the possibility of brown damp which would certainly result in a flame-out. At that late date, there was only one option and we took it. We decided to take the uncalculated risk of a sudden decline in fuel supply. There are times when such critical decisions can make or break an entire project. We were also under additional pressure because of the time element.

Two hefty football players accompanied the supply to the privy and stood guard outside to assure that there would be no loss that would cause the project to be aborted. There was some concern that the donor might try to escape through the seat hatches. After some rapid-fire mathematical calculations involving algebra, trigonometry, and calculus, it was determined that mass exceeded available space by several inches. And that was before the advent of mind-boggling computers. That route didn't lead to anyplace that anyone in his right mind would want to go, anyway.

When they brought him back, he looked as if he were beginning to develop some scientific feeling for the project. He became enthusiastic to get on with it.

When he got inside the windowless space lab which did double duty as the locker room, he lowered his corduroys and his long drawers and hopped up on the table without a bit of assistance. He carefully got into position on his side and tucked his knees toward his chest, with the propulsion device properly exposed.

Signals were coordinated and a last minute check made before starting the countdown.

Murphy's law had not been enacted yet, but the principle was in place. The ignition expert decided to roll a cigarette with his right hand and lit it with a double farmer match held in his left. That was the precise moment when the subject shouted "Now!"

The ignition device was hastily shifted from the cigarette and into position. There was, at that very instant, a resounding "B-r-r-r-r-r-r" as the igniter contacted the fuel supply.

The fuel supply was adequate, the head (?) pressure must have been just right. The darkened room was illuminated briefly by a bluish-yellowish flame that shot out in one direction for at least a foot. The device, entirely surrounded by a fat little freshman, shot out in the opposite direction until it hit the door, which gave way under the force of the impact.

The corduroys and long-johns down around his ankles surely must have slowed him considerably, but he did the ten yards or so to the shower room before the lab door slammed shut. And that was before we knew about door-closers. He did carom off one wall that stepped out into his way.

Secrets will out. Someone had squealed and the student body had sent representatives as observers. The only real accident in the experiment was when one of the onlookers became too curious and stepped too close the orbital path. He lit on the floor, but had no injuries.

During the scientific evaluation period which immediately followed the lift-off, the subject said that the ignition expert got the firing device too close to the gas port when he wasn't paying enough attention to his job. That was what caused the high-up hot-foot. We tried to get him to volunteer for one more try in order to determine the exact cause, but I suppose he figured that once was enough. We were already pressing our luck. Some of the sessions with unruly students didn't last that long.

Please don't get me wrong. I'm all for equality for women, but there are times when they could easily interfere with the progress that men can make. That was one of those times.

If we had tried to involve even one or two of the girls in that project, it would have failed miserably, although one girl would very likely have been smarter than all the rest of us put together. Integration of females into that initial experiment could have set the entire space program back another twenty years.

As it was, the project did get off the ground. Neil had to have a solid place to put his feet when he stepped down from the landing module.

We discovered how to put a moon into orbit.

I don't want to give you the wrong impression. All of that account is hearsay from a reliable source. If you accuse me of being one of the experimenters, I will deny it. I would not have thought of doing anything to upset the principal and the coach. But the other hush-hush rumors that circulated at about that time supported the claims of the person who made this remarkable disclosure to me.

Another Story From Anna

The young lady who told me the story of the little house out back which lacked the proper cutouts liked my telling of the tale so much that she told me another.

She was an inquisitive little girl. She was not really ornery, just mischievous. She pestered every adult she could find to tell her where they got the eggs that appeared on her plate every morning. They lived on a farm, so they did not come from the super market.

She could not receive any satisfactory answers from anyone. They continued to put her off by ignoring her. That was the wrong way for them to respond to Anna. She was only four, but Anna had an analytical mind. She decided there must be some mysterious source and de-termined to learn for herself. And what Anna determined to do, she did.

She watched and learned that there was some link with the chicken house. She disappeared one day just after lunch. She wasn't missed for nearly two hours. Then the alarm went out. The adults hunted high and low. They didn't look where she was.

She stood scrooched over for four solid hours watching one hen on the nest. She had guessed right! When the egg popped out, she popped herself into the house and announced proudly, "I know where eggs come from now."

I asked her if she went on eating them just as she had before she became so smart. She did.

How to Beat Your Wife
(or Husband, as the Case May Be)

I just heard on television (where else?) that a large percentage of espoused or sorta-espoused humans get their jollies through wife-beating. That is hard to believe.

The commentator didn't mention husband beating. That omission may have been intentional, since she was really a commentatoress. Okay, so just what is the feminine gender of commentator?

That big figure almost slipped by me while I sat with my jaws ajar. I learned some sixty-plus years ago that it is more difficult to learn with your mouth open, but the figure that bounced off my tonsils on its way to my earpans sounded a lot like forty.

I was so flabbergasted that I may not have heard correctly. I do have a congenital defect that causes me to not hear well. I call it "the seventy-two-syndrome." It adversely affects other things besides hearing.

I don't have any idea where the pollsters polled, but it wasn't around my bend of the hill. I was reared in the hills where most poll takers wouldn't set foot and our telephone was one of the crank-type twenty-party lines. A pollster wouldn't have needed to ask questions if he had just taken time to listen in on some of the chatter. Our ring was a long and a short.

Men in those parts were real he-men, most of them hairy-chested and as tough as dried hornbeam.

I never knew of a man who beat his wife. We had one or two in the general area who had a sorta-wife. They didn't pound or stomp on those, either.

That may have been because most of the females were real she-women, rugged, hard-working, and as tough as cured hickory. I'm not too sure of any hairiness. They could work in the fields alongside their men when necessary, run into the house to prepare the meals, and flop into bed at the end of a hard day.

They must have been ready to fuss and fight or whatever it is that couples do after they retire in the evening. They surely didn't have much time for it during the day.

If wife-beating had been prevalent in our backwoodsy area, I surely would have heard of it. I heard of everything else that happened, most of which didn't. If rumors had been true, we would have made Peyton Place look like a Sunday church service.

Girls today aren't nearly as pretty as the girls were when I was a young man. Maybe that same congenital defect has taken a toll on my eyesight, too. But if a male (preferably single) kissed a pretty girl (single preferably) on her back porch, rumors of a future wedding were bruited about before their lips had a chance to cool.

By the time of the third evening of smooching (not necessarily consecutive) the mother of the bride-to-be would be carrying a bouquet of daisies with roots attached. Those were just in case the bride's father's white shotgun was a little too effective and the reluctant groom would wind up pushing up same.

We knew what could happen when kisses became too passionate. We were raised on farms where cows and sheep did it all the time.

If affairs, pre-marital, extra-marital, and inter-marital were as rampant as rumored, spouses of both sexes must have forgiven the trespassers, even if forgetting was out of the question. Some may have received a blackened name which was never mentioned on the party line, only over the back gates. I never saw one with a blackened eye which could not be truthfully explained by some other phenomenon.

I must admit that when it comes to wife-thumping, I am the absolute voice of inexperience. I do beat my bride of fifty-three years every time I can by catching more fish than she does. That may be because I always sit in the rear of the boat where I can run the motor.

She does have some consolation. Hers are usually bigger. And she rarely has to paddle.

And I'll be doggoned if I'm going to teach her to play golf.

Grandpa B. (Thrice Removed)
and s-e-x- Education

I'll bet good soft greenbacks that you just wouldn't believe some of the things I've been seeing recently on television.

I watch the news channels on an irregular basis. That is where I take all my adult classes in s-e-x education. They certainly do intend to enlighten the viewers.

You probably noticed that I spelled out the "s" word rather than just write it right out. You will probably want to know the reason.

One of the things that I heard on my second favorite news channel about two or three weeks ago was that only about eighty-three percent of our high school seniors don't know how to spell. That leaves about seventeen out of every hundred who might recognize the word if they saw it in print with the letters all together.

Seeing it in print right out there in front of everybody like that other word the kids print all over the bridges, rocks, trees, and handy store fronts would very likely start them to tee-heeing. They would have to explain to the other eighty-three why they had developed a sudden attack of giggling. That would set the entire class into an uproar. If there is one thing in this world I don't want to do, it is to disrupt a class of seniors where one or two students might be trying to learn how to spell s-e-x. They must be having trouble

68

enough learning to spell the simple words.

I know what the mere mention of the word would have done to my eighth grade class on graduation day. And our ceremony was held in a country church. I can be absolutely positive about the reaction, since I was the only member to graduate that year. The nineteen-year-old boy and the eighteen-year-old girl had dropped out before the big day, leaving a lone twelve-year-old to carry the class banner. There was no mechanical nor electrical connection between their quitting.

Spelling was one of my stronger points. I learned how to spell that other word before I was four, too, but if I had printed it in big red letters on the Mail Pouch sign on the barn, I would have had a bigger and redder thing to sit on for a week or two.

Back then we didn't have a National Endowment for the Arts to back me up. I probably didn't know what the word meant anyway, but every time some older kid saw it, he laughed.

I figured if I spelled s-e-x most of them wouldn't know what I was writing about, since that many of them lack the ability to spell. But they might recognize it by sight.

I have been puzzled for some time about the real reason for that condition. I have reached the conclusion that one factor might be that they are spending so much time learning about s-e-x they don't have time left over to learn how to spell all those other words.

Things were different in my earlier times. We had

to learn how to spell it while doing our homework.

This paragraph doesn't have one earthly thing to do with spelling, but I wanted to stick it in to show you that they haven't been spending much time on geography either. They had a pretty little girl who had just graduated from high school on television the other day on that same channel. I think they were trying to embarass her. Someone asked her where the British Isles were. She didn't know. They then asked her where Europe was. She didn't know that either. I can only guess which class had been taking most of her attention. I'll bet it wasn't History.

I want to talk to you for a minute or two about the s-e-x education which our youngsters are receiving in school. That is to sort of lay the groundwork for what I want to tell you about my Great-great-great-grandpa Berdine and his s-e-x education.

I think you should know about some of the things the kids are being taught already in the schools as well as a couple of things which have been proposed. I can solid guarantee you that if it is introduced as "Sex Education" the kids are going to learn it. Some of it is simply not true. It may be hard to remember facts, but the human mind rarely forgets what it learns that only imitates facts. I know from first-head experience.

One of the things that kids are now being told by way of television, the classroom, and one political aspirant who was a big shot in the medical profession in her home state (which shall remain anonymous in this account. I wouldn't want you to find out who she is. You might want to ask her embarassing questions.) is that it is okay to have all the "safe" s-e-x they want.

If I can remember that far back with any degree of accuracy what some of my contemporaries told me when I was in the upper grades of elementary school and in high school, what they want is an indeterminate and incalculable mythical quantity. I don't suppose teen-agers have changed all that much since I was one only five or six decades ago.

What some of them got is something else altogether. Today it can be fatal. Back then it was just plain and painfully unhandy. If you don't count consequences.

I'm not one to put much faith in what people tell pollsters like Dr. Kinsey and Jim Comstock. For those of you who don't remember Dr. Kinsey, he interviewed a few women and came up with some stories about the undercover life of the American female. Jim Comstock said he did the same thing in Richwood soon afterward. They either talked to a lot of people who weren't too careful with the truth or my memory is a lot worse than I ever suspected.

The pollsters today have come up with a whole new set of figures which indicate that I must have been born about sixty years before my time. Unless they were questioning a few prevaricators, too. Some people will lie about their love life who wouldn't tell an untruth about anything else. Witness the wild stories in the scandal sheets. They must feel the need.

71

I heard that one of our esteemed leaders (the female politico hereinbefore mentioned) had told her teenage constituents that it is okay to sleep around, but not to get married. Now that is what I call sound advice. All sound and no substance.

I have no idea what her husband thought about that statement. Come to think of it, I don't believe that I heard her husband mentioned, not before, not during, and not since. She may not own one.

I also heard on an earlier newscast that the kids are receiving "free" condoms, presumably from the government. Those guys think that if they are holding your purse strings and doling out a million or two here and more there while building their own little nest egg with the overflow that what they are giving away is free.

One of our esteemed leaders was recommending that the girls get their fair share by carrying their own supply. Something like going Dutch, I suppose. That was some more sound advice. It was probably to assure stricter quality control. If government-issue condoms are like anything else they pass out, the girls and boys will need all of the quality they can scrape together.

I suppose that carrying your own little jar of "butterflies" wouldn't be much worse than some of the older women in my backwoods neck who toted their own snuff.

If all that hasn't kinked your wig, another newscast said that one school had hired a practicing prostitute to teach the kids "how-to." I hope it wasn't a hands-on learning experience like disecting frogs, grasshoppers, and night crawlers.

Another newscast that may have been a propagandizing effort to support the other one mentioned above hinted that the kids are being told that using a condom provides a safe barrier to the AIDS virus, or HIV. That is pure hogwash.

If you doubt the veracity of that last sentence, I'll share with you what I heard on that news channel day before yesterday.

It reported that the British, bless their souls, had been fooling around and had come up with a new condom made of polyurethane that was touted as being a good deal safer than the old latex material. Stop and think about that for a minute or two.

If the polyurethane model is only safer, they must mean that it is still not entirely safe. It must also be a statement which supports my critical article of more than a year ago. It must be saying that the latex or other suitable substitute material is not nearly as safe nor as foolproof as our youngsters and two or three of us oldsters have been led to believe.

The broadcast mentioned the presence of "pinholes" created in the latex versions during the manufacturing process. A pinpoint-size hole in a piece of thin latex would look to a virus about like a Chesapeake and Ohio Railroad tunnel would look to a groundhog.

That doesn't take into account the rupture rate. One estimate that I read somewhere or another placed

73

that unreliable figure at something between thirty and forty percent. I haven't seen a serious study by Consumer Reports that compared the various models like they do with cars and videocassette recorders. But give them time. They will.

My Grandpa B. (thrice removed) didn't take s-e-x education classes in school. He didn't take any other classes, either, but that's beside the point. He never learned how to spell nor write his name, let alone how to spell s-e-x. He very likely could not speak much English when he first came to this country before 1750.

He must have known how to load, aim, and fire a musket and how to count coup on the restless natives. He may have been pointing his shootin' airn at some of his former neighbors from the Old Country.

He was sweet-talked or shanghaied into fighting in the later stages of the Indian Wars. That is one of the wars you don't hear much about in History any more. Maybe because the kids are spending too much time learning to spell s-e-x.

That war began about the time that a handful of Englishers poked their longboats into a river mouth on Chesapeake Bay and started stealing cigarettes from the natives. The war ended more than two hundred fifty years later at a little out-of-the-way place called by some people, "Wounded Knee." Historians try to separate it into a lot of little bits and pieces so that you can't figure out what actually happened. They may be too ashamed to tell.

Grandpa B. was active in the later years of that part which we mistakenly call The French and Indian War. The British still call that portion The Seven Years War. They were fighting with everybody.

Grandpa was also in Lord Dunmore's War, which should have been included in the earlier set-to, since it was still a part of the war for empire.

Grandpa B.'s last service was in The American Revolution, where he got to practice on the same big red targets he had been hiding behind earlier and which were so hard to miss.

Somewhere along the way he managed to learn a thing or two about the process and method of reproduction and propagation of the species. He may have received a part of his s-e-x education from hearing the dirty jokes while sitting around the campfire with the older boys. Maybe some of the fellows were school teachers too.

After he got tired of fighting, he decided to try some other recreation. He wangled, wooed, and wed a lady who was considerably younger than he. As nearly as I can compute, Grandpa must have been pushing forty.

He taught her everything he had learned at Valley Forge and while swimming the Delaware. She taught him what he had missed. They proceeded together to produce a family of thirteen little Berdines.

Shortly after the birth of the thirteenth, she became ill. A neighbor sent down two of his daughters as indentured servants to work off a debt to Grandpa.

Grandma's fever was fatal.

Grandpa had just turned seventy-five.

He liked the way one of the girls fried his sowbelly and corn dodgers, so he married her. She was twenty.

Grandpa started giving her s-e-x education classes and they produced another dozen before she got her diploma.

I guess what I am really trying to say is that in spite of a lack of advanced degrees in s-e-x education, a few of the old-timers managed to find out something besides how to spell it. Some of them managed to increase the population by leaps and bounds while they were fumbling around trying to find their way. A few of them may have jumped a bit too far and too often.

If some of them could have foreseen what their great-grandkids would be taught from the time they enter kindergarten until they get their fingers firmly wrapped around the skin of a wayward sheep, they might have been a little more careful.

They might have spent a lot more time fishing.

But I doubt it.

Warlocks and Witches

Not everybody gets to know a real live warlock or witch in their entire lifetime. I did.

Most of those who have been touted as one or the other were actually neither. Unless you want to count those who practice their voodoo religion in some of our neighborhood South Sea and Caribbean islands where anything is possible.

The neighbors, whether they are cursed or uncursed, have a tendency to believe that anyone who appears to be a little different really is. Most of us in this day and age rarely tend to believe that our next-door neighbor is a witch. We might think something else about her that is worse.

One problem with neighbors' opinions is that they get peddled from door to door rather cheaply. They sometimes become fairly widespread.

That is what happened to one particular neighbor up in our neck of the woods where everyone's next door neighbor was more than a quarter-mile away. That was in the short direction. If you looked north or south, that stretched to more than a mile on the Yankee side and more than two on the other.

The other was the direction where the witch's house was located. There was one house between. The witch's house was a half-mile farther on.

There is an old saw that hasn't slipped my mind which says, "Little pitchers have big ears."

That guy must have been talking about kids. When someone mentioned witches or warlocks, our ears grew to the size of philodendron leaves.

I had overheard all the stories. Some of them more than twice. I never walked past her house on moonless nor moonlit nights. I made as few trips as possible past there in the daytime.

I was forced to go into business for myself at the ripe old age of eight. There may have been considerable influence from a female to whom I was closely related. She didn't have enough money to keep me shod. I went to work to buy shoes to cover my outsized feet after the first frosts hit when tootsies were apt to suffer.

I tiptoed summer barefoot along the mountain tracks and called on every household within a radius of six or eight miles. One of the tracks went within rock throwing distance of the witch's house. I solemnly swear I never even picked up one.

I seem to recall that business was a little slow back there in the last year of the roaring twenties. They had dribbled down to a fizzle in our area by 1930. If it had been brisk, I probably could have afforded shoes without risking life, limb, and heaven only knows what else.

It must have been very slow on that trip. I stood in the dirt road in front of her house, scuffling my toes in the dust to get the grime off of them. I bit my quivering lip, shoved my shaking hands into my overall pockets and marched to her back door. That's where all business was transacted in those parts. I couldn't do anything about my knocking knees, but they banged together on every step anyway, even while standing still.

When she came to the door, I could only stammer. My silver tongue had suddenly turned to lead. My sales pitch stuck right there where my Adam's Apple would eventually take shape.

I was known all over that end of both townships. My father had been known even more widely, but for different reasons. Everyone who should have been feeling sorry for himself felt sorry for me. Now that is what you call really poor.

She exclaimed, "Why, it's little Billy Berdine." It has always amazed me that so many people with my forename are called "Billy" until they grow to about six feet when they change subtly to "Bill." She looked at my Larkin Company catalog and gave me a nice order.

She invited me into her kitchen. I was still too scared not to go. She sat me at the table and proceeded to pile a big bowl of raspberry pie, still warm, drowned in cow's milk with the cream still in it.

One look at my bulging bones convinced any mother or would-be mother that I was seriously underfed. I wasn't. The bulging muscles just above my belt didn't show up until several years later.

That was just my first trip to her place. Her kitchen was spotless, which was saying something for that time and place where sheep, cattle, and hogs were on our care lists. There was always some carry-in and it made extra work for the housemother.

I learned that she was a good cook too.

I have no idea where her husband was or if he was still living. She had an adult daughter and son living with her. As far as I know, I was the only company they ever had. They reveled in my frequent visits. So did I.

She did make "witches' brews"--the same kind everybody else in those hills made and kept simmering on the back of the stove or tightly corked and out of the reach of the younguns.

She was one of the kindest women I have ever met. Her daughter and son would play ball with me under the two big buckeye trees in the front yard. The game was limited to catch. When you get that old, running bases gets to be more work than play.

I am beginning to believe the folks in France made a whopper of a mistake when they kindled the big fire under Ste. Jeanne d' Arc. She wasn't a witch--just an overly bright country girl who made the yokels jealous.

I am also beginning to have some serious doubts about the wisdom displayed at the Salem trials in this country. Those victims may only have been a little ahead of their time and slept with their eyes open.

Just like I do.

Run Into the House, Kids
the Earth is Shrinking

I hear and sometimes see some of the oddest things on television. Once in a while I learn something. I just learned the other day that scientists have just now discovered that the earth is shrinking.

I'm not sure whether it was on one of the news channels where I take all my adult education classes in advanced science or on the Discovery Channel where I take adult education in all kinds of current affairs and some which are un-current.

I don't know about your place, but the earth isn't the only thing that is shrinking around my house. My un-long memory is at least two lengths ahead in that race, but I can still remember learning that fact in high school. I graduated from there cum-barely about fifty-five years ago.

Our principal was a man of principle who had made a name for himself as a collegiate basketball player. The earned name was "Zip." He was a bit different than your run-of-the-boards basketball player today when anyone under seven-foot-nine can find nothing better to do than pull splinters from the end of the bench with his union shorts. He was about five-four and faster than greased lightning. He couldn't have swung on the rim with both hands to save his neck.

Most players today can look down into the net without standing on tiptoe, and they still swing on the rim.

It must be fun.

I was six-three tall and one-ninety-seven wide and could run almost as fast as a Jersey cow just before milking time. My big problem was my feet. One kept getting in the way of the other.

We had a terrific relationship. He appreciated my empty brain which was bellowing for knowledge. He insisted in the last four semesters of my fast-fleeting school days that I take a math class and a science class in the same opening period. I don't know yet how I managed to get straight A's in those doubled-up classes, but I learned more when I was working three times as hard to keep up than I did when I was coasting.

It was that principal who started me to thinking about our shrinking ball. He started me to thinking about several other things as well. His body may have been miniature but his brain was giant size. My shrinking memory hasn't forgotten Duane Woods, better known as "Zip."

A few years back when I was beginning to think seriously about retiring and going into some more-unprofitable line of work, I went to a southern state to interview a sales rep to take over the territory I had been working to develop. I had a call waiting when I arrived at the motel.

Washington had already jumped the gun and hired him, so my interviewing and evaluating was unnecessary. I had already scheduled a breakfast meeting. We met.

The only subject I could think of on the spur of the moment was my retirement. Sometimes my mind works like a steel trap--a week or two after when I think of something I should have said. I told him I was planning to stay in that favorite of all the several states I had visited, West Virginia.

He was in love with Florida. When I told him I had ruled out Florida several months back, he asked why. I explained that the population had doubled in the last decade and would likely do just about that during the eighties.

He wanted to know what was wrong with that. I often have trouble saying things in a few words, but my answer was one word. Water.

I went on to explain that the aquifer was being depleted. Florida was about to start falling in. One more good dry spell would do it. He looked at me as though he expected me to start foaming at the mouth any minute.

He obviously thought most West Virginians were a few degrees off plumb and the rest of us carried watches that weren't wound too tight. He thought I had totally lost my bubble.

He called me three weeks later to ask, "How in the world did you know?" I told him that one of two things was inevitable. When the water was removed, the ground would collapse or salt water would infiltrate the aquifer. Both have already happened.

I should probably take credit for being brilliant, but

anyone who has read my little pecan-filled pieces would know better. All I was doing was applying what Zip had told me more than forty years before.

The earth is shrinking. The crust is still cooling after all those billions of years the scientists keep throwing at us. Any hillbilly knows that heat causes bodies to expand and cooling causes them to shrink.

See how simply it can be explained.

The world moves aside and lets pass the man who knows where he is going--except at intersections and on curvy two-lane roads.

Our Spring

I wasn't watching television this time. I was tossing and turning in my bed, trying to coax the last sheep to run a little faster so he could chase away the recurring thoughts of my distant and somewhat shady past. Not criminally shady, mind you. Just dim shady.

I don't know how I got started on thinking about water, but suddenly right there before me in my mind's eye was our old spring.

It was a pretty good spring as springs go, but it had a couple of faults by nature and another one or two by hillbilly engineering.

The water came right off the limestone that underlaid those hills and hollers. It was so hard that you had to chop a hole in it with an axe to pour it out of the bucket. That was in the summertime. I have often tossed a cake of Mom's homemade lye soap at a tubful of it. The soap, as strong as it was, bounced right off the top more often than not.

I'd almost swear that you could take a bath in it without getting your feet wet. Ears rarely got wet during the ablutions. Mom would swear to that.

That water was as sweet as any I have ever tasted. It was always the same temperature winter or summer. It was so cold that it made your teeth hurt and your eyeballs ache if you swigged too fast.

The spring never froze over in the harsh winters we thought we had back then. Ice did cover the lower end of the spring drain in the coldest weather and the watering trough which stood about twenty or thirty feet below it got a thick layer of ice on all sides. I can't recall that the pipe carrying the water to the trough ever quit running nor can I remember the top of the trough freezing completely over.

We had one winter when the temperature sagged to thirty-six below zero. That was on our Fahrenheit thermometer that we bought at Bill Finlayson's five and dime store. It was sometime before those foreign words, Centigrade and Celsius, had infiltrated the language of us common folk. Some scientists used them, but you had to be a high-school non-dropout to convert from one to the other. If you had a book and knew which page displayed the double formulae which we never remembered.

Another fault of the spring was that it got roily with every hard rain. Downright muddy was what it was. As soon as it started to sprinkle, the small army of kids and as many of the adult officers as could be rounded up ran to the spring and filled all the milk pails, water buckets, crocks, and pans. The first one to the spring got the job of dipping. Looking back, the frantic filling and toting must have been hilarious to a bystander, if there had been one. They were all busy filling their own buckets and pots. It wasn't nearly as funny then.

The spring was located on the steepest and tallest hill in that area where all of the land was sort of sidling. Flat ground was anything with less than a five percent tilt. That may be why so many of us lost our marbles. They rolled off.

The house had been built years before indoor plumbing became the standard in those parts. The engineers who plotted it forgot that water won't run uphill without a little help. The house was about four feet higher than the spring which was about forty yards away. That may have been why we captured every drop of rain in barrels.

Our Saturday baths were taken in rain water in wet weather and in spring water in dry. We had a real bathtub. The water would run out, but it wouldn't run in. We toted water and heated it on the wood-burning stove. The guy who carried the water got to take his bath first. That is the reason my arms are so long. The buckets stretched them.

The same water was used by all ten of us or until the tub got so full it had to be drained. We all knew what everybody else did in the bath water. Why do you think I fought so hard to be first?

I left that spring nigh on to fifty-five years ago. The last time I saw it more than thirty years ago, it was still going full tilt. I wonder if it still does.

Given the way we have been depleting our aquifers, I doubt it. One of these years we humans are going to wake up looking backward to see where all the water went and why our once-fertile cornfields have suddenly turned to deserts.

That may be when we go the way of the dodo.

It's a Crude, Crude World

It may seem hard for you to believe, but I was trying to watch television last evening with nothing on my mind but fun and pleasure.

I had bypassed watching all of my normal channels such as C-Span, and CNN. I was too late to watch the news and other goings-on on the BIG channels, NBC, CBS, and ABC, where I usually find the grist for my word mill. I grind a good deal of it into pure corn.

The TV guide from the newspaper (I'm too cheap to buy the real thing) was just out of reach, so I flipped to the program listings to see if I could find anything that might not insult my ears, eyes, or intelligence, not necessarily in that order.

Wouldn't you know that the little picture in the upper corner of that channel which advertises up-and-coming attractions was using language that I wouldn't use down behind the barn. I was afraid to peek.

I hastily hunted for the mute button on my remote. But I was too late. I had already been. The filth passed his and her lips before my un-nimble fingers could flick over the keyboard and find the right button.

We quit going to movie theaters many years ago for the same reason. The screen would be filled with a good picture which was relatively clean. I watched for a "G" rating. "PG" means Parental Guidance Recommended and both of mine have been dead for years. It was the previews which turned me off and made me keep my hard-earned change in my jeans. You had to sit through them first. They were mostly X-rated.

My mother wasn't exactly a prude. My father wasn't even close, especially in his younger days. My education in special languages came by hiding around the corner and listening to him talk to the horses and not hiding and listening to my mother's brothers talking to me. They tried to teach me everything they knew. They probably thought that it was a demonstration of three-year-old intelligence to be able to swear like a mule-skinner.

None of them spoke French, Spanish, nor Italian, but I was fully conversant in mule-skinner-ese before I reached that ripe old age. By the time I was four, I was addicted to lye-soap mouthwash the way some people are addicted to cigarettes or whiskey or worse.

I was just four when my first teacher brushed my britches with a stout hickory for practicing my foreign tongue on a pretty little coed in the first grade. Unlike many coeds today, she blabbed to the teacher.

The teacher must have heard the words before because punishment was swift and painful, especially at the seat of learning.

I'm not sure whether it was the sudsy soap, the frequent dusting of the dirtiest part of my bib overalls, Mom's shaming me, or the threat of more bodily harm that moved me from the well-driller shop talk to plain English, American Style. I like to think it was my own superior intelligence.

Subsequent events and circumstances have led me to believe that it was probably none of the above.

I was baptized by an itinerant preacher when I was barely twelve. Just after he preached a sermon on the vitamins and minerals and other healthful stuff in a glass of water.

My baptismal font was at the juncture of two fair-sized streams. They were fed by dozens of runs, branches, rills, and spring drains. I had wandered all of them and nearly every one of them had a privy standing spraddle-legged over it. I think it was more the solemnity of the occasion rather than the water which cleansed my soul and my mouth at the same time.

My mental attitude changed when he said, "In the name of The Father (first dunk), and The Son (second dunk), and The Holy Ghost (slam dunk)," I was born again without the filthy tongue in my head. I still told funny jokes.

I firmly believe in the First Amendment, almost as firmly as I believe in the second, etc., but there should be some provision to protect those of us who don't like to hear the filth which comes out of the mouths of boobs and babes who apparently think that it makes them sound "macho" and "fe-macho."

We don't go to ball games any more, either.

How Some Hillbillies Use Corncobs

If you have hung around these hills and hollers as long as I have, you have undoubtedly picked up a few odd uses for some products of nature.

Practically everyone who lived in these mountains before the roads mysteriously evolved into hard-top by-ways and thoroughfares has made use of wild fruits, nuts, and plants. Some were used for food, others for medicine, some for both.

One such product is the lowly corncob after all the grain has been peeled from it. We normally shelled ours by hand, although we did have a hand-operated field-corn sheller for what we fed the chickens.

The cows were fed the "nubbins." Those were the small ears. We chopped the larger ears with a hatchet and fed the bits of cob and corn in the manger feed box.

The bare cobs have been used for any number of things down through the years since the Aztecs' ancestors started plucking the few odd-shaped grains from teosinte.

Teosinte is the grass which is supposed to be the ancestor of corn. I have read that the harvesting of the few grains was indirectly responsible for the growth of the magnificent cities of the Ancient Mayas, Olmecs, Mayas, and Aztecs.

We who look at corn cobs from this side of John Deere and Luther Burbank find it hard to believe that our corn could have come from that skinny little stem of grass. Corn cobs got a lot bigger and more useful somewhere along the way.

I once made corncob pipes from the corn like we raised when I was a kid. I stuck a piece of "pipestem" into a hollowed cob and sold them like wild at Pipestem State Park before I ran out of good cobs and couldn't find any more except the skinny kind.

Scientists jumped on to the corn ears after Burbank moved on to a bigger job. They made the grains longer and the cobs skinnier until today it is nigh on to impossible to find a cob big enough for any practical use to which hillbillies were apt to put such miracles of nature. They must have been more interested in eating than in puffing. They may not have realized what they were doing to people back in the hills.

The pipestem I used in my pipes is the reed of the Spirea Alba. It once grew near Pipestem, W. Va. in patches so thick that the rabbits had to run through them backwards in order to find their way out again.

It grows in many locations, some of them far removed from Pipestem. There was once a huge patch near Buckhannon, W. Va., but U.S. 33 gobbled most of it. It grows in boggy areas in Pennsylvania, New York, and Ontario. Those are the ones I know of.

A related plant, Meadow Sweet, grows in those locations and others. It grows in England where they used both fresh and dried leaves in the old days under mats and rugs to discourage fleas and other household pets. It was also used to deodorize rooms that must have smelled all the way from the dirt floors to high heaven.

Back to the corncrib. I have a friend who has been a hillbilly all her life. So far. She knows more about old-timey mountain customs than I do. She is India Brown, manager of the gift shops at Pipestem State Park.

This is how she told me she uses corn cobs. She still uses it on occasion.

Corncob Jelly

18 red corn cobs. Break cobs into one inch pieces and cover with about four cups of water. Let boil for 30 to 45 minutes. Take three cups of the liquid from the pan. Add one box of Sure-Jell. Let come to a boil again Add 5 cups sugar. Let come to a boil. Time for about 5 minutes. Skim. Add one-half teaspoon vanilla. Spoon into jars while still hot.

Test jelly by putting one teaspoonful on saucer and chilling in freezer.

Enjoy!

And don't go around telling people that I won't share my goodies.

Footnote: After the article appeared, my oldest reader, Mrs. Faye Garrison of High Point, NC, wrote and told me that her mother used a similar recipe to make "maple syrup." She flavored it with maple sugar. Mrs. Garrison remembered that it tasted like the real McCoy.

sex-**Gate**

You will notice that I put the first part of that other hyphenated word in the title in lower case. I did that so the eighth graders who read my column would not be so likely to notice and also to put that part of the word in its proper relationship to its importance to the subject of this article.

I have been spending too little time in front of the tube these last few days. I have been so busy peddling and autographing my book that I haven't been able to keep up with the news as well as I should have.

I try to watch somewhat more than my allotted share of the programs on C-Span, NBC News, CBS News, and the two cable news channels. I try to keep you informed of all the important happenings on those sometimes dry programs so that you can spend your time more fruitfully watching Oprah, Sally, HBO, and other such worthwhile programs. Those might excite your imagination, widen your horizons, and titillate your tendencies, but they don't do a whole awful lot to improve your mind.

Besides all that, you may be missing quite a bit of news that has turned out to considerably nearer the truth and a whole lot racier than the put-ons put on those programs. You surely don't believe all that stuff which participants seem so reluctant to tell, do you?

What little news I have seen in the past week or two has been sandwiched between the reports of alleged activities of a former governor of Arkansas when he was allegedly overactive while allegedly sandwiched between the sheets. Not alone.

Two of Arkansas' finest let the female cat out of the bag, so to speak, when they started telling tales outside the Governor's mansion and rooming houses. The big difference between the two dwellings seems to be the abscence of the red lantern on one or the other. I have not looked at the front portico of the White House to see if that one has been taken down.

Governor C. (not to be confused with Governor C. of W. Va., Governor C. of Del., Governor C. of Minn., Governor C. of N.Y., Governor C. of Mo., Governor C. of Pa., Governor C. of Fla., or Governor C. of S.C.) may have had a good reason for jumping the fence on a few occasions. I just don't know.

He should have been more discreet if he didn't want the word to get out. He is learning that you just can't trust anyone to keep his or her mouth shut.

It seems a bloomin' shame that the same Democrats in the House, the White House, and the backhouse who wanted to tell everything they didn't know about Clarence's fooling around with Anita while he was trying to work up enough nerve are now trying to pile all the covers they can lay hands on to conceal the Governor's activities when he apparently got up more than enough nerve.

The undercover activities are not the most important factors in this story.

The important factor is the attempted bribes and cover-ups. Alleged, of course. One report said that YOUR tax dollars were again being used to buy silence. Those were to be spent to put the tattletales in a position in the Federal Government where they wouldn't dare say too much. Money makes strange bedfellows. So do politicians.

There is allegedly a strong movement within the heirarchy to discredit the two State Troopers. If that doesn't sound familiar, refresh your memory about the firm denials of the extramarital affair with the Powers woman. The big lies she told turned out to be the big truths.

The House tried to impeach Nixon because he tried to cover up the theft of a few unimportant papers. I'm not sure if he ever had his fingers on them. If the women who were allegedly involved with the governor were virtuous, the Congress should remember that virtue once damaged can't be cured by slapping on a couple of Band-Aids or basting with needle and thread.

A cover-up can't be covered up with sawdust as an old alley cat I once knew personally was apt to do. The stench still came through the clean pine scent of the shavings, even after he covered it up with his paw.

Teenagers Can Get "In the Family Way"

I want to warn my regular jolly readers that this article is not funny. Every time I start thinking about some of the mess(es) we have made for ourselves and our progeny, I become un-funny. I have a hard time recovering my sense of humor after a session like the one I am reporting here.

I just saw on television another startling revelation or two. Television is where I get all my adult education in illegal violence, illicit sex, and immoral politics. It is, in fact, becoming more and more difficult to get anything else on television.

You will not likely believe this, but a small town high school in Texas had the nerve to oust four cheerleaders from their coveted high-profile positions because they became pregnant. I'm not sure those all happened at the same time, but the evidence appeared almost simultaneously.

That wasn't the amazing part. Cheerleaders and other high-school girls have been doing what comes naturally for nigh on to two hundred years now. They were doing it before that, but we didn't have high schools in which to practice cheerleading nor football teams to egg on with our "Rahs" and high-jinks.

The amazing part was that some woman from New York who had likely never crossed the border said that it wasn't the cheerleaders' fault. It was hers.

I would like for her to explain to me just how she

97

got those four girls pregnant. On national television. I can't help but wonder if she got in the family way, too.

I'm not much of a bible-thumper, but the Bible tells us at least a part of the problem. It says, "Whatsoever a man soweth, that shall he also reap. For he that soweth to his flesh shall of the flesh reap corruption; but he that soweth to the Spirit shall of the Spirit reap life everlasting." If we substitute "humans" for "man," we have the answer.

That woman in New York may have meant well, but she has been brainwashed and misguided. Each of us is responsible for his own actions. My mother had a saying for it when she admonished me before I set out in pursuit of some pretty girl. That was most of my limited circle of acquaintances of the other gender. I can't recall ever seeing one that wasn't pretty. She said, "Remember who must sit on the blister if you get burnt." She wasn't talking about backing into the Burnside.

Our socialistic, atheistic, agnostic, and immoral ethos has lead us toward moral and national decadence. It can never lead us to anything else.

I do not mean to say that any and all intimate contact between the sexes is wrong. I am only saying that there is a time and a place for it. Under the bleachers or behind the goalpost is not the place. The school years is not the time, unless it is preceded by a simple ritual called marriage. My personal opinion is that fourteen is too early for marriage.

98

The "liberal" media, especially television and movies, promote this mindset by attempting to glorify uncontrolled and uninhibited inhuman behavior by humans. That propaganda is not limited to sexual contact. Incomplete minds tend to believe the trash and garbage which is the product of other incomplete minds and to accept it as normal and acceptable behavior.

We have allowed pseudo-intellectuals to alter our brains by their loud-mouthed presentations of the "modern" philosophy. It is not modern. It is as old as The Garden of Eden. It is merely a rehash of the same old misrepresentation. The major problem is not that it is being presented as an acceptable ethic. The major and basic problem is that so many borderline mentalities accept it as ethical.

Any person, whether he is a teenager or an octogenarian, who submits to this far-left philosophy is headed for destruction. We used to say, "Headed for hell in a handbasket," but only the older people would know what the term means.

Those presentations and their acceptance by various and sundry persons are far more destructive to society than all the handguns and/or automatic and semi-automatic weapons that all the manufacturers lumped together can ever produce. If the do-gooders want to do something which would really benefit our society, they should concentrate on the basics, not the symptoms. The acceptance of that bassackwards philosophy and its promotion by the electronic and cinematic media is one of the basics. It should be sharply curtailed or stopped completely.

My own efforts toward reducing the portrayals on television and the big screen are the most effective, but only if all concerned parents and grandparents get into the act. I simply do not attend movies and I refuse to support the supporters of such trash on television by refusing to patronize any sponsor of the programs which promote it. That is sometimes difficult, especially when you reach for the remote control at the first utterance of some filthy four letter word and find that your reflexes aren't what they used to be.

All violence depicted on television or in the movies is not bad. Kids and irresponsible adults like the Congress and the President should be made aware of the real horrors of war. The old "Cowboy and Indian" movies didn't seem to bother us too much. We knew they were make-believe, especially the parts about the Indians. The songs about the cowboys didn't seem to bother us too much either.

The "songs" of today which promote cop-killing and other assorted violence are another story. They prey on the minds of every teen and young adult who has already been led to believe that it is not his fault that he wants to go out and shoot up the neighborhood. It is the fault of everyone else.

You probably won't see reprints of this article in many of today's newspapers and magazines. It might cut down on their source of sensational news stories if we were successful in ending the proliferation of violence and promiscuity. That would fly in the face of all that is holy to the hoi polloi, to hear them tell it. But on the other hand, the common man is more of a myth than the Bible, which the intelligentsia claim is only a collection of myths.

Let me get back to the beginning of this article. The school board did exactly the right thing. The rules were already in place. They were not made ex post facto. The girls knew the rules. They surely knew the consequences of sexual intercourse (often mistakenly called "sex" or "love." Another case of using a misnomer to soften the harsh facts).

The males in the fiasco should be punished as well. There must have been some. I did hear that it was impossible to tell who they were. That fact wasn't emphasized, but guess what it means. Guess why it wasn't stressed by the media. It would never do to mention that when you run through a patch of blackberries, it is difficult to tell which thorn scratched you. If you think that the reason it wasn't mentioned repeatedly was to protect the girls, guess again. It would never do to condemn promiscuity.

The female New Yorker's statements are typical of the free-sex fraternity. We had better begin to mature as a society. We had better learn that some farmer on the backside of Elk Mountain was not totally responsible for the bombing, the riots, nor the four cheerleaders becoming pregnant in Texas.]

You Can't Catch Any Fish That Way
(a Letter From Canada)

Sandy,

I am writing this in pencil and in wobbly longhand for a few simple reasons.

Margy and I are in Northern Ontario again on one of our futile fishing forays. That alone should explain a lot of things.

I tried to pack my portable typewriter in my shirt pocket to try to smuggle it across the border without paying the seven percent national goods and services tax (a.k.a. GST which can also mean "God Save Toronto").

That tax is similar to the one that some of our more thrifty legislators want to put into effect in the U.S., but we are going to call ours GSP. I don't know whether those initials mean "God Save the President" or "God Speed the Payments." Up there, the tax hits everything imaginable at least once and most of it twice. It is like a number of our taxes that fool people into believing they only pay it once or not at all.

I gave up on trying to sneak the machine into Canada because it made another unsightly bulge somewhere north of the equator which is my belt line and some sharp-eyed customs inspector might have become even more suspicious about my odd shape. I have noticed a few of them casting inquisitive glances at the unsightly bulges that God hid in various odd places under my shirt. I gave up after several tries and packed three pencils instead. Those fit the interstices.

102

We have been almost fishing only once since we arrived here on my birthday on May 11. That was the day I passed the allotted three score and ten and started living on borrowed time.

We missed the first two days of the season because Margy picked up some funny bug as we sneaked through Pennsylvania and New York. She brought it across the border unnoticed and nurtured it until it interfered with the normal flow of things. It gave me a good excuse to stay inside the cottage, since I have given up on trying to swap her for a new rod and reel. The original cost was only two dollars, but maintenance costs over the past fifty-two years have been somewhat exhorbitant and prospective swappees balk when I want them to absorb the overhead.

We actually arrived in Canada on May 10. That was the day they broke all records for hot. We arrived here in Shiningtree on May 11 at 12:30 a. m. and went to bed in the cottage that our friends, Al and Wendy Craigie, had made ready for us. They operate The Country Store and Lodge and know of my odd behavioral patterns, having put up with me before.

The weather celebrated my birthday on Tuesday by providing a beautiful spring day. Sunshine, moderate temperature (in Celsius, of course--they don't understand the temperatures that Fahrenheit gave us), and no black flies yet. We unpacked and toted and enjoyed the beginning of another delightful trip. Our eighty-first, if Margy hasn't lost her notch-stick.

The next day we decided to do a little exploring. We drove to a back road that was supposed to take us to a new fishing hole that was almost inaccessible. We didn't find it. We did find some monster moose tracks and some more monstrous wolf tracks. That was as close as we have been to a wolf on this trip. They are gentle animals and will only eat you if they are hungry or something.

We also saw several bear tracks. Some of those were huge. Bears won't eat you--well, hardly ever--but they may hug you to death. That was all we saw of the bears, too.

The next day we took the six-horse Evinrude and made the seven mile trip up a long creek to the lake we had decided to fish on opening day. We jumped eight beaver dams in the first three miles. Then the water became too deep for beavers and we cruised in under a full head of gas. The recent rains and snow-melt had swollen the stream until it was passable.

We started the trip in beautiful sunshine and shirt sleeves. I told you before that I try to foresee all sorts of things. My law differs from Murphy's in that I claim that if anything can't possibly go wrong, it will anyway. It did. Fortunately, I packed three wool shirts, two rainsuits, a down vest, and extra wool socks. Those were just for me. Margy had her own.

We got to the lake just after lunch, which we ate while sitting in the boat and watching the ducks do whatever it is that ducks do when they think no one is looking.

Then the wind picked up. If there is one thing in Canada that you can never depend on, it is the weather.

We didn't take the boat out on the lake. It gets rough when the breeze jumps to about thirty per and that jonboat doesn't have much tolerance for rough seas. Neither does Margy.

We started the trek back down the creek (north) and we hunted for every piece of brush that might break the wind, cold, and sleet that had set in. That is hard to do when the tallest trees average less than three feet high. The wind was in our face and right off the polar ice cap. That slowed the forward progress of the boat and grew icicles on our West Virginia noses. Even the ducks turned tail and flew.

Margy put on all the extra gear and what she could pilfer of mine. I still have blue spots on my head from her pilferage. She still got cold. I am the he-man type so I didn't really notice the sudden drop in Celsius. And pigs don't have curly tails.

That was the last nice day we have had. But the weather will change. It always does.

The bug sneaked in on Margy on Friday night sometime after midnight and about four minutes after the starting whistle blew for opening day. I know, because she shook me awake after eight tries to tell me she had to go to the bathroom, which was inside and just around the corner from our bedroom door. She may have thought we were sleeping in the tent.

She fed her pet bug for the next two days. It is just as well. It gave me a good excuse to stay inside the cottage, which may have been the smartest decision I made during the entire trip and for several weeks before. The weather turned nastier. It rained. Then it snowed. Then it snowed some more just to prove that it hadn't forgotten how. Then it rained again. Then it froze. We got up at five on the third morning, all set to try it, but the four inches of snow on the ground and the twenty-nine degrees on the thermometer sort of cooled our enthusiasm. The minus one on the Celsius scale looked even worse.

Late on the third day, after the snow had melted from the two inches of rain that washed it into the lake, we decided to give it a try. We went to a small lake just down the road a piece to try for a few fish to fry for breakfast. I drug the boat down to the water, loaded it, watered the minnows, and started the engine. Margy brought the lunch and my four quarts of weak coffee.

We hurried down the lake so that no one would see where we were fishing. It is a secret hole that only a few people know about. Even fewer catch fish there. We made a hasty trip past there on Sunday and counted twenty-two vehicles. We may have missed a few.

Just as soon as we were out of sight of the sightseers we slowed to a troll. I picked up a nice pike, which we call Wendyfish. She likes them. We eased on down the lake to the rapids and crossed the portage that no one knows about. The trail is worn about six inches deep, but that may be from moose crossings, although we didn't see any moose tracks. Unless you count the two-legged kind that wear lapel pins and funny hats. We saw several tracks that could have been those.

We stopped to gather a bag of reindeer moss from a huge chunk of the pre-Cambrian shield. The weather was still fairly good. We clambered down from the rock and started to unlimber our rods for fishing just as it started to rain.

I still caught enough fish for breakfast and lunch and had a couple to throw back. I beached the boat and unpacked to head back to camp.

I pulled the boat up to the edge of the road and stood erect to sort of catch my breath. When you suddenly turn seventy-one, you suddenly notice that some things are shorter than they used to be. Breath is one of them. Days are another, except when you are 'way up there on the Arctic Watershed. Years are a whole story of their own.

I shifted my considerable weight and caught my foot between the transom and a knot on a rock on which I was standing and started the long journey downward that ended with me sitting in the narrow space between the seat and the transom and wetting my breeches from the pain that showed up when the small (?) of my back collided with the sharp edge of the seat. If grown men could cry, I would have sobbed. I knew that the crack I heard and felt was another broken back. I figured that I had exceeded my lifetime allotment of two.

I was afraid to move and afraid not to. I wiggled my toes inside my kangaroos. They worked. Then I tested a leg. Then the other. Then I said, "Oh!, -----." and rolled over on to my knees. I got to my feet, loaded the boat and gear in the back of the truck and drove back to camp, bragging all the while about being in good shape for an old man who had just dumped two hundred twenty five pounds of bone and blubber backwards across the sharp edge of a boat seat, and downhill at that.

The next morning I left all of the crowing to the roosters, all of which were smart enough to stay at least two hundred kilometers farther south. My old friends, the muscle spasms that fell me, did.

It interfered with my fishing. The additional daily rain got the water too wet to fish and the sand roads too bottomless to negotiate in two wheel drive. We spent my aching-back leisure time talking to some of our Canadian friends.

They are worried about what they are going to do after Mulrooney resigns and they will be left without a leader. I tried to console them by telling them not to worry, we have been getting along without one in the states and not noticing a whole lot of difference. I haven't been catching any fish there either.

I have been doing a little thinking between games of solitaire and while my back is too sore to fish or anything about something I heard on television just before I came north. Since my book has already sneaked into

Korea by the back door, some Chinese scientists may have sneaked a peek and done some serious study that may offer some support to my Un-Theory of Evolution.

Some of my readers may have heard the same newscast. It was on at least one channel where you can hear just about anything if you can stand to sit through a few days of stuff that isn't fit to watch.

It seems that some scientists somewhere way off to the East--or West, if you happened to be pointed that way--have now determined that we did not come from apes at all, thereby agreeing with a part of my book which makes the same claim. They, too, are claiming that Darwin's theory is a lot of hogwash, although they aren't saying it in so few words.

As you know, Darwin came up with his theory about thirty years after he had spent his fishing trip unfishing and wandering some deserted island in the Pacific watching wild canaries. It was long enough afterward for him to forget some of the more important details.

The scientists over there had more modern equipment that was far more sophisticated than Darwin's pair of fogged-up bifocals. They had the distinct advantage of a complicated electronic device called a tape recorder.

It is amazing how some seemingly minor everyday occurrences can prove to be such major scientific breakthroughs. It makes one wonder if we all might be spending too much time talking and writing and not nearly enough thinking.

It was just such an everyday event that led to this unprecedented scientific conclusion about the ancestry of the human race.

Some farmer who had been raising chickens for the chow mein market decided to go into BIG business and started raising turkeys instead of dominickers.

If you know even the slightest thing about turkeys, you already know that they are the stupidest creatures that ever walked on two legs. There may be an exception or two.

As soon as he had made the changeover, he discovered that he had a big problem. The young turks would not go to sleep at night and get their rest so they would grow up big and plump.

He displayed a touch of genius when he came up with a solution that human parents have used for centuries to get the little ones off to beddy-bye and into dreamland. He decided to tell his poults bedtime stories.

He didn't know how to talk turkey, but he had a neighbor who had a dozen or so adult turkeys that hadn't fulfilled their destinies.

He tiptoed to the next town, talked to the turkey tutor, taped the turkey talk, tucked the tape into his trousers, and trotted toward his turkey tent.

He decided to listen to the tape before he played it to his turklets to censor out any words that might not be fit for their tiny ears. He may have been watching some American TV on the sly.

I can't figure out what happened next and they aren't telling. I can only guess that he must have punched the rewind button or turned the tape upside down or something. When it started to play, it was in reverse.

Lo and behold! It was right then and there that he discovered that for all these many years, turkeys had been speaking Chinese backwards. He reached the only logical conclusion and couldn't wait to tell his friends in the scientific community. They could only agree and take all the credit.

Humans evolved from turkeys. There could be no room for any doubt, since the turkeys were already fluent in the area's most prominent language. Backwards at that. The apists were wrong!

I couldn't handle being outdone by some chicken farmer in some remote corner of the farther East, so I came up with an even odder origin for humanity.

My observations were made while sitting at the breakfast table in a cottage in back-country Canada.

I had a little extra time on my seat because of the conditions affecting my wife, weather, walleyes, back, and fishing stated earlier. Just as I finished my bacon sandwich made with French bread and my bowl of instant oatmeal porridge made with hot water, I noticed a tiny black spider sitting in a hastily built web near my right elbow, patiently waiting for me to toss it a piece of bacon and a slice of toast. It must have lodged there so that I couldn't miss it.

I know that its house must have been built overnight because I had placed my deck of cards there shortly before midnight. I gave up trying to win at solitaire without cheating at about that time. I hadn't let any cobwebs grow on those cards during the evening.

That spider wasn't a black widow, but it may have been one of the widow's unkissed cousins. It did start me to thinking about the black widow and its traits and characteristics.

There is a logical scientific reason why the black widow is called by that name.

The female has a bright red spot on one side and a bright red hourglass-shaped spot on the other, but for the life of me I can't remember which is on top and which is on the bottom. The males have even shorter memories than mine, but for a different reason.

The male has orange spots where the female has red ones. His spots aren't usually as large, since he doesn't have as much room for them, her being female and all.

The red spots on the female are there so he can find her in a dark corner. The orange spots on the male are there so she can find him as soon as he is finished finding her.

All the activity causes her to be famished. She latches on to the nearest tidbit, which happens to be her impromptu spouse. She commits husbandcide.

Did you ever stop to think how much humans are like spiders? Other than the number of arms and legs, of course.

The big difference is that human females take a little longer to destroy the male. They don't normally eat them. They just worry the men to death. If you don't believe me, take a gander at the statistics. Women outlive men by seven or eight years. On the average.

And you thought all the time that we came from apes.

God made another big mistake when He made new parents. He should have made them as smart at eighteen or nineteen (those are the late-comers to marriage now) as they are when they become seventy-five and have grandkids running all over the place.

Life Afta NAFTA

(or "What's It All A bout, Will ie?")

Now that NAFTA has at last passed, I have been spending a few of my waking moments watching and listening to the Opponents, the Proponents, and the Exponents on television hash and rehash the future and perhaps one or two little things from the past, Senator Bob Packwood's past notwithstanding.

I still don't know whether I am fer er agin NAFTA. I really don't suppose that it makes much difference now. It didn't seem to make much difference before when I didn't know whether I was being proed or conned. Not any more than it didn't when anti-NAFTA labor unionists and Perotites appealed to their Congressmen who I thought were supposed to be representing them rather than telling them what was good for them.

The most vociferous group from the above three classifications (O's, P's, and X's) has been the newly-become Ex-ponents. I have been at a loss to explain to myself or to you how those Congresspersons (I used the neuter here because I am not at all sure which ones have been -ed) could possibly be so opposed to NAFTA and then suddenly shift position to become supporters. Maybe the under-the-table hand that held the cash was quicker than the eye.

The Ex-ponents who were talking have been making speeches right and mostly left. The speeches have been rather enlightening, considering the fact that most of the speak-easies appeared to be somewhat in the dark. For those of you who would rather watch shows like NYPD Blue and Roseanne to get your political education, you just wouldn't believe what you have been missing on C-Span and the two new news channels, CNN and Headline News. Some of the stuff on those makes Murphy Brown look like a Sunday School teacher.

Most of the Ex-ponents I saw on any of those channels weren't saying anything. They had their chins buried just below their collar buttons. I jumped up seven times during one program to adjust the color on my Sylvania. The tube had suddenly turned a glowing pink. They all looked like a little boy I once knew who wet his Sunday-go-to-meetin' knickers one cold January morning on his way to church.

Three or four of them at least did manage to look the CBS eye right in the eye and tell not only their constituents but everyone else who couldn't reach his remote control quickly enough why they turned coat. I thought the reasons sounded reasonable enough.

The outstanding one to me (and I have come up with some pretty good "reasons" of my own) said that he sold his vote because he got to stand beside Willie the Wisp to have his picture taken. He didn't say if he got to kiss him on the cheek.

115

He can have the negative for a few million of your dollars and his promise not to tell.

Another had gumption enough to get a little something worthwhile for the tomato farmers in his state. The way he explained it, Mexico had to promise unfaithfully that they would not ship any of those tomatoes grown in that cheap fertilizer they use down there to any place but someplace else.

What I would like to know is what they did for the peanut farmers. We have one who retired a few years back and I heard a rumor that he is having a terribly hard time growing enough goobers to keep body and soul together. Somebody else did say that his welfare check is substantial.

I thought I understood another to say that he had done a good thing for the seamsters and seamstresses in his state by excluding textiles from the agreement. I don't know why the West Virginia and Michigan representatives didn't think to exclude cars and coal, not necessarily in that order.

What I want to know from that guy is whether we will still be able to get Genuine Mexican Velvet at the discount stores and flea markets. Will we have to shell out more pesos for a picture of Elvis or Marilyn now that the south-of-the-border wages are going out of sight, maybe to as much as one-sixty-five an hour? Will the eagle still fly or will he have to sit on that scrawny limb all day? Overhead items for artists like brushes and paint will probably skyrocket as well.

People collect those things, you know. Some of the collectors are even the opposite sex of the paint-ee. Some of them here in the hills don't have a mantel to hang one over nor a window to throw it out of.

As I said earlier in this article and even earlier in another article, I don't know enough to make a judgment call on NAFTA. I probably wouldn't know enough if I had time to read the fifteen hundred pages of fine print.

I did notice that a few businessmen, big and small were reported to be absolutely for NAFTA. They stood staunchly behind it from almost day one when that other fellow was in the White Hotseat. His name has slipped my mind. I have not detected among them one single hemidemisemiquaver, let alone a whole quaver. Lee Iaccoca was right at the top of the heap, but you should remember that Lee is a used car salesman. And I didn't mean "used-car."

Most (I didn't really count, I'm just guessing) of the big and small businessmen in the metropolis next door to mine were in favor of NAFTA. One of those guys will top two-fifty, one wouldn't go over a hundred pounds with his feet wet.

I have an intestinal feeling (I didn't want to use that other vulgar expression in front of the kids) that I can trust those guys. I know a few of them on a handshake and Howdy basis and they seem to be a pretty decent bunch of fellows, But one of them sells used cars too, along with a new one every now and again.

117

About the only complaint I really have so far about NAFTA (there may be another or two later) is the fact that Willie the Wisp spent millions of your and my tax dollars to cut all the used-car deals. If NAFTA is so good for everybody north-north (Canada), north-south and south-north (US), and south-south (Mexico), why did some of our representatives have to sell their souls for a few shekels and why did Willie use our shekels?

I've seen a few horse trades in my day. What I would like to know is who, besides the Canadians, is left holding the dirty end of the stick. Somebody always gets stuck with the blind mule.

One guy did admit after plugging NAFTA for all he was worth that we might lose only a million or a million-and-a-half jobs, but the loss would be temporary. Thank God, it will only be temporary.

"Temporary" is an indeterminate amount of time, defined more specifically by whether you are gnawing on neck bones or pigs' feet or eating ham and pork chops.

I hope NAFTA lets all of us start eating high on the hog.

Putty Tats and Puppy Dogs

There should be at least one more right removed from the citizenry before President Clinton is impeached or otherwise impelled to leave with his tail between his legs.

That is the right of individuals to allow their favorite dogs and cats to run free and fill everyone else's petunia patches and potato plots full of natural fertilizer of somewhat dubious benefit.

People here in West Virginia would never turn an unwanted dog or cat loose to freely roam the countryside, but there are any number of folks in our neighboring states who think nothing of bringing their strays all the way to the Mountain State where they can feed and forage on our huge overabundance of birdies and beasties. We don't call it "Wild and Wonderful" or "Almost Heaven" for nothing.

Dogs aren't quite the natural killers cats are, but if they become feral dogs, they have to eat somewhere, even if it is behind Dairy Queen or Shoney's. All the cats I have seen were already feral, including those that were housebroken enough to walk across the kitchen cabinets or the kitchen range stalking a bowl of Charlie Tuna or Puss 'n' Boots.

I knew of one cat who was experienced enough or smart enough to stick one paw out to feel the eye on the electric range to see if it was too hot to trot on. I would guess that he had received a hot pussyfoot at some time.

People in this country have inherited a strong superstition from Ancient Egyptians who believed cats were sacred and it brought bad luck to kill one. It seems odd to me that we still have cats but there is not a single Ancient Egyptian to be found. Living, that is.

They may have been right. It will bring you more bad luck than you can shake a lawyer at if you kill either a dog or a cat and the SPCA finds out. You would be better off shooting your neighbor's wife. He may have had her too long anyway.

It is all right to turn them loose to hunt and kill or to starve. Who pays any attention to a stray cat or dog? Only the recipient of such an unwanted gift, especially if it raids the house of your nest of house wrens which you have been guarding with your water pistol.

Cats, either feral or tame, and I use the terms loosely, roam the woods and the neighbors' yards on a seek and destroy mission against songbirds, pet rabbits, squirrels, chipmunks, and it is hard to tell what all else. They leave the undigestible remains in places where you normally walk or work the soil with your fingers. Some of it is hastily covered so you won't know it is there until two seconds too late.

Dogs are different. They only dig holes in flower beds, douse the shrubs with defoliant, and deposit calling cards on your front stoop. They usually don't leave anything in the holes except bones. The foliage only dies as high as the dog can reach while standing on three legs. The droppings are carefully placed just outside the door where they will trap an unsuspecting bare foot. Doggie doo will squish between the toes of a shoeless foot like you wouldn't believe. That word is from the voice of experience.

Most of you would not know that feeling, but here in the hills there are still some of us old timers who never got out of the habit of going unshod.

What this country really needs before Willie the Wisp retires from politics forever if we are serious about reducing crime is a strict licensing law on dogs and cats. There should be a waiting period of at least thirty days (and nights) for the FBI and the SPCA to run a background check on prospective owners to see if they are financially and mentally capable of owning a pet.

There should be a new agency created to monitor the beasties continually to be sure they are kept on their owners' premises where they can poo and pee to their little hearts' content.

The agency could assign serial numbers and place an exorbitant tax on the food they use to manufacture their ammunition. If it will work for guns, it should work with cats and dogs. Think of how many jobs could be created, since there are more dogs and cats than people. The bureaucracy could outnumber welfare workers.

I'm one of those people who love both dogs and cats just so long as they do their business in their owners' houses and yards.

Vive! Vive les carnivores!

Federal Deficit Reduction

Guess what I have been doing again! Oh, What the Thunderation, I'll just go ahead and tell you. I've been watching C-Span again.

Boy! Can you ever get an education on C-Span! And the only time sex gets violent or language gets out of hand is when you see stuff like Anita accusing Clarence of taking personal liberties with her person.

She told it all right there in front of the Senators who were about to pass judgment on the would-be judge. You could tell they were interested by the way they kept inching forward in their pews every time she opened her mouth. They could hardly wait to see what she was going to reveal next. Ted Kennedy's eyes bugged out until you could hardly see the bags, but that might have been the grease paint.

C-Span nearly always leaves enough to your imagination so that you can draw your own conclusions. In some cases you can even write your own ending. Except for Bob Packwood's alleged sexcapades. I'm not sure that any of those ever reached a conclusion.

C-Span C's all, Nos all, and Tells all. Just like it is. Uncensored and uncut, as long as it is fittin'. It may trudge pretty close to the edge every now and again, but it never gets quite as raw nor quirky as some of the soaps, Sally, Vicki, or Oprah. That observation is made on the basis of hearsay and the ads they sneak in on the news channels. I've never watched any of them and intend to keep right on not watching as long as my two eyeballs can separate trash from truth. I have a cataract, so that might not be a finality.

What I saw today was taped yesterday and had absolutely nothing to do with the above. That was written as a come-on. Today's show was as dry as last week's corn pone, but it sure was informative.

I had started an article about three or four weeks ago on the subject and it looked almost as funny as the program. It had less humor than the time one of my un-rich uncles held a church funeral for his prized fox hound, with preacher and all. (The preacher was an avid fox hunter too, so he did the eulogy free of fees.). I'm not sure what they served for refreshments at the wake, but the jug looked suspiciously familiar.

I had no idea at the time that the Congressmen (this time I could pretty well tell) had as much trouble as they did in trying to sneak their bill past the money-savers. I decided to go ahead and finish it since it seems worthwhile for all good and devoted contributors to Federal Budget Reduction (hereinafter referred to as FDR's to comply with Government Regulations for Initializing Programs, Etc. or GRIPE) to read.

Do you who live in the backwoods or the back alleys of this dis-United States still believe that the recent whopper of a tax increase was ever intended to fulfill its stated objective of reducing the Federal Deficit? If you do, you haven't been paying attention to what your Congressmen and your Senators have been doing while your back was turned.

Congressman Timothy Penny, Democrat, Minnesota and Congressman John Kasich, Republican, Ohio in this past session proposed a budget reduction plan bearing the name of The Penny-Kasich Bill. Don't ask me why a funny name like that. It did propose cutting spending almost across the board by one penny on the dollar over the next five years. For those of you who have mislaid your slipsticks or calculators, that comes down to a one-percent cut, give or take a slash or two in some rather sensitive places. The savings would have amounted to ninety billion dollars.

If you are anything like me when it comes to money, you have absolutely no idea how much a billion dollars is and don't know who to ask, even if you could get up enough nerve. I don't know how many bushels of West Virginia Golden Delicious Apples or Idaho Spuds it would buy, but it must be more than two or three. If you would rather compute in corn, it would probably buy enough of those funny brown jugs or fruit jars to tipsyfy everybody in Richwood.

Seriously, that is only about one-fiftieth (that's right, you didn't read wrong, 1/50 or .02) of the National Debt.   It probably isn't proper to capitalize, but anything that big deserves some recognition, if only from me. I may be the only one that notices.

That would be the equivalent of having a 250 year mortgage on that little house out back with no interest. You could never pay it off.

That ninety billion figure doesn't mean that we would have that much left over after all that saving on paying for peanuts we can't eat nor ship, wheat we can't grind into flour, corn we can't squeeze, shootin' airns we can't carry, homes for wayward adults they won't live in, and subsidizing drug dealers, drug users, unwed mothers of seven or more accidental births, freeing felons and studying such things as perverted and subverted sex as practiced by flies, frogs, fish, and some animals with less legs. It just means that we would only go two-hundred-eighty-billion in the hole each year instead of three-hundred-billion. Those are rounded figures.

Guess what happened. The proposal kept getting shelved, tabled, or stuck on the back burner until the last week or so of the session when it was covered up with stacks of paper. When it finally did get to the bar, the Congresspersons (this time I wasn't sure at all) were either too tired or too inebriated (that's a fancy word for tipsy) to care. It went down to the ignominy of defeat faster than Max Schmeling in his second go-around with Joe Louis.

The Clinton Administration and its liberal left-wing hangers-on pitched a hissy when it was presented. They stormed Capitol Hill with threats and pockets lined with your tax dollars like a foreplay of NAFTA, only with less fanfare.

Television and news commentators were almost as ecstatic as they were over the passage of the Brady Bill and NAFTA, but not nearly so vociferous. They didn't want you to know that their Willie the Wisp had led you down the greenbrier path again. You might become disillusioned and think he had lied. Again.

If you can remember as far back as the summer of '92, you may recall that he was in favor of reducing the deficit. He promised.

It was reduced--from what they intended to spend.

Some of you may remember that the tax increase was to do that, along with the accompanying cuts. He promised. Some of you may remember that the "rich" were going to pick up the tab for all the good things you were going to get just for voting for him. The "middle class" wasn't going to be hurt. Not much. He promised.

The cuts didn't happen except in OUR defense. We still supported Russian defense. The taxes did. Boy, did they ever. If you haven't felt them yet, wait a few more weeks. You will. I promise.

Historical note: The administration is now asking for another tax increase to offset all the cuts they made earlier. Congress never met a tax increase it didn't like. My own opinion, stated, is that Congress is bent on destroying the United States through fiscal mismanagement. It is working, and unless the American people wake up to reality, we needn't worry about the Constitution and Constitutional Rights.

We won't have one.

The Queen and I

This article doesn't have a lot to do with politics and absolutely nothing to do with television as do most of my other articles, but don't panic. It is about one of my all-time political favorites and the time that I............. Oops! I almost tipped my mitt by putting the punch line right there.

The story goes back a piece. More than thirty years, if you want to fix an approximate date. Two of the principals are long gone. My mother and her brother, Jim, were killed in an automobile accident only two years later.

Mom and Jim had spent a few vacations with us in West Virginia. Jim had become a fisherman in his later years because of some evil influence from a relative who was addicted to trout fishing. That relative would fish for other species when he could get them to bite.

We had caught a few fish on those trips. That is another story that I might tell one of these days when I am doing my old-age reminiscing.

They had spent considerable time with us at the bottom of one of our gorgeous gorges peering upward at the narrow strip of blue where eagles used to soar. It was where the sun made its trip from mountaintop to mountaintop in a little more than an hour on normal days and in a little less than that when it was in a hurry.

Every time I called for them to come south for a visit, they figured that I must have treed a few trout or lassoed a couple of nice bass.

This time I called about two or three weeks ahead of time to make arrangements for a visit. I told them not to bring fishing rods. We were going to see the sights and stay overnight. I didn't tell them where.

They arrived on schedule. They had not brought their Sunday-go-to-meetin' clothes. They figured they were going to see some more of our beautiful hills that pop up out of our hollows every now and then.

We piled into the Ford and started south on 250 and then east on 50. I drove across Laurel, Cheat, and Allegheny Front while they oohed and aahed. When we wiggled our way across Capon Bridge, I told them we were on our way to Washington, about another hundred miles away.

Back in those days, Washington was still in its innocence outside the capitol grounds and you could move about in comparative safety. I wouldn't attempt the same thing today for all the catfish in Buffalo Creek.

After some excited discussion, they decided that they would not likely see anyone who would recognize them the next time, so what they wore would be good enough.

The nearer we came to Washington, the more they became at ease. They were enjoying the scenery from the rural highway through the rolling farmland and the occasional plantation with their miles of stone fences. If someone hadn't picked and piled all those rocks, Virginia wouldn't have a patch of soil big enough to grow a tobacco plant.

We stayed at a motel in Mt. Vernon and I bounced everyone out of bed before daylight. I can rarely keep a secret very long, but I managed to keep that one. Someone in some position of relative unimportance had tipped me off to a possible trip to the U.S. by Queen Elizabeth II. The trip was to see how the descendants of some of her ex-countrymen were faring in that colony across the water. It had once been named in honor of her ancestor, Queen Elizabeth I, but the boundaries had shrunk faster than a pair of new denim jeans in hot water until there was only a remnant still known as Virginia.

I had some advance notice of the route of travel for that day, so we made a hasty visit to a couple of our lesser national shrines and then high-tailed it to the shelter of some small bushes at curbside. We took up all the space between the shrubs and the curb.

When Mom asked why we were waiting there, I told her that my favorite monarch would pass within arm's length. If Mom hadn't been a sturdy farm girl, she would have pitched a hissy right then and there.

My informant must have had access to some inside information because the Queen did come by there--very slowly.

I don't know if she waved at anyone else, but she looked directly into my baby blues and smiled. I crumbled. I could lift more than 750 pounds back then but I didn't have enough strength to lift my arm to touch her hand. She knew.

No, I didn't faint or otherwise make a fool of myself right then. I'm not sure about later.

I hustled them into the brand-new Ford and proceeded to join the entourage as it moved into the Virginia countryside. My vehicle was the last car in line, but what the heck, there were only seven ahead besides the Queen's limousine which also carried the President.

When I told my Canadian friends about how close I had been to their sovereign, they said, "Oh, go on with ye. You didn't."

But I did.

So did Mom and Jim. They told the story over and over. They were the envy of that farming neighborhood where people are still good country folk. I guess she must have waved at them too.

I couldn't swear to it. I was too busy enjoying the brief encounter between the Queen and me.

The Queen may have forgotten it. But I haven't.

AIDS (HIV) and Other Bugs

I saw it on television the other day. It was aired on all of my favorite news channels except the one which tells us what Congress is or isn't doing. It was a repeat of what I had been saying ever since I learned to spell AIDS with capital letters.

Biting bugs can aid in the spread of AIDS. Cats are one of the culprits called "carriers." Cats carry fleas which nibble on the cats. Fleas bite humans. Voila! The flea-bit humans get cat-AIDS.

My wife and I spend a few weeks on each of two or three trips to that country to the north where everyone speaks two languages, often simultaneously. We usually wind up in Northern Ontario on one side or the other of the Arctic Watershed. The primary purpose of those trips is to fool a few fish into biting so we can bite them back. Sometimes our plans "gang aft the way we want." Meaning we catch one on occasion.

We take at least forty-four dollars worth of Off! 100% DEET with us on those trips and use it more freely than some people use toilet water. We have coined a phrase to describe it rather than say Off! 100% DEET each time. We just say "Canadian Cologne."

Off! DEET smells just like all other 100% DEET-- terrible. If you use the proper amount, no one can tell for sure that you haven't bathed in the last week or two. You always smell the same before and after your shower. If you don't, pour on a little more Off!.

The reason for the Off! is obvious. The mosquito is the national bird of Ontario, barely nosing out the black fly for top honors. The only reason they top the black fly is the decline of black fly populations as soon as the sun gets hotter than -----. The flies can't stand the heat, so they get out of the kitchen.

Mosquitoes thrive on sunshine, stagnant water, and red or blue blood. They seem to be color-blind. Peerage is subject to punctures just like other people. The biters congregate in swarms so thick that you have to shift into four-wheel-low to plow through them.

The publications I have read on the subject say that only the females bite. Those articles convinced me to the extent that I repeated it (not verbatim) in my book, "The Berdine Un-Theory of Evolution and Other Scientific Studies Including Hunting, Fishing, and Sex" (which is available from West Virginia Parkway Authority Shops, Pipestem State Park Shops, The Hillbilly Book Shop, Bookland, Jackson Square Book Shop, Patronik's Books, Stuyvesant Square Book Shop, Stillwell Book Shop, and from me, the guilty party, among others).

I have been trying ever since to separate the males from the females. I have not achieved any notable success. I find it difficult to tell one from the other.

I won't stoop to letting them bite me, although a few of them have when I was. If you have to make a hurry-up trip to the bush in an emergency up in the Arctic or near-Arctic, you will find that the mosquitoes and black flies have already explored the area and set up house-keeping. They have several fast-food joints scattered around in the bush, one of which is moose antlers in velvet. (See chapter on "Moose" in book barely mentioned above).

When you drop your drawers behind some scrawny tree, it is like a neon sign on a back-country road saying, "Eats, Cheap." Black flies and mosquitoes arrive in droves before you can get properly positioned for the business at hand. They land and start probing at any spot not doused in DEET. That one rarely is. Even when you apply it properly, all the sitting and shifting in boats, etc. wears Off! off.

You can stay busier than a one-eyed cat watching nine rat holes swinging and swatting. They can turn an expected pleasure jaunt into a miserable outing in less time than it takes to say, "B-z-z-z-z-z-z."

Every locality I have visited from Florida to the Far North has had mosquitoes. One reason I like West Virginia well enough to stay here is that it has less mosquitoes than any other place I have been--in mosquito season, that is.

Ontario adds black flies for your inconvenience. Every place I have seen mosquitoes, someone has already trained them to bite humans. Every place that I have seen black flies, they are worse than mosquitoes.

They are in Quebec, but there they bite in French patois, which everyone else calls Quebecois for short. They are just as plentiful as in Ontario.

I have read somewhere that a female mosquito feeds only once in her short but nasty lifetime, so she could not carry the HIV from one animal to another.

I know that is a whopper. I have seen and felt mosquitoes and black flies which didn't get to finish their entree because of a sharp slap at their rear. I have seen hundreds of them dodge an ill-aimed slap just as they were sitting down to dinner. I would almost gamble my hard-earned welfare check that some of those who flew away to bite again did.

The AIDS experts (?) have been telling us that the malady cannot be spread by mosquitoes and black flies. I wonder if they are the same experts who were telling us a couple of years ago that it couldn't be spread by fleas. They should go to more circuses.

I also wonder what else they haven't been telling us. I wonder even more about what they have, especially about the holey condoms they have been advertising with all the free samples.

An Intercepted Letter

Shiningtree, Ontario
May 17, ---------------

Dear Fran and all the other pleasant people we left behind in Princeton,

Here we are again! Up there in that country where everybody speaks two languages, one of which isn't Spanish and the other isn't either and where the fish grow bigger after the evidence has been eaten.

I would have written as soon as we got here, about 11:00a.m. yesterday, but the ink froze in my pens. Those were in the inside pocket of my insulated underwear. I like to keep two or three handy for autographing books. Besides, the mail had already run.

It runs on Monday, Wednesday, and Friday of most weeks (holidays excepted). The rest of the time we look at the pictures in the old catalogs and the 1987 Newsweeks.

There isn't much else to do and the natives start waiting for the mail to run just after the new mail sack is nearly empty. They use a sixty-gallon sack with a hefty padlock to bring in the three letters and the discount store ads (usually four, but some weeks those are used for fuel in the Burnside in the Toronto Branch of Canada Poste).

We have been here almost twenty-four hours and have had only two snowstorms. The first caught us on the way in (without our unaware). It snowed six inches in less than two hours. That made towing the boat hazardous to our health, but the only place in the ninety kilometers where we could pull off was a Provincial Park--closed. I got behind an eighteen-wheeler driver who had windshield wipers on his tires and did pretty well until he tried to lead me astray into a roadside swamp. He got it under control about a foot shy of utter chaos. His and mine.

The swamp was good-sized and I had thoughts of the big rig and my little rig going out of sight. I would have felt funny if some coal miner in some distant millennium had dug me out and unknowingly run me through a coal processing plant.

These Canadians can tell time fairly well, but they don't know beansoup from apple butter about temperature. We stopped in Sudbury to eat an early breakfast and the TV said it was three degrees. I almost froze fast to my chair before I went outside and found that what looked like a "C" behind the "3" on the screen must have been a "7."

At least one of them has some trouble with time. I told the cottage owner that we would be there Wednesday. She thought I meant "Wednesday." I had to explain that "Wednesday" is an indefinite article and it really was Monday.

Tell Kathy B. that she wouldn't like it up here at this time of year. The geese haven't come north yet.

I told her about the S.O.B.'s (Sand On the Beaches) and the G.O.B.'s (Gooses On Beaches) earlier.

The G.O.B.'s walk all over the S.O.B.'s and leave G.O.B.'s footprints and other telltale signs on the S.O.B.'s. Believe you me, when the G.O.B.'s go back into the water to wash their feet, they leave behind a bunch of dirty S.O.B.'s. Polluted with goose footprints. But it keeps the drinking water cleaner.

We haven't been fishing yet. We got here a full five days before the season opens to give me time to put my rods together. I'm getting old and forgetful and I sometimes go fishing without line on my reels. That makes casting easier and you don't have to clean as many fish. I only did that once a long time ago, but there is a female relative who keeps bringing it up every whipstitch or two. One of these days I'm going to surprise her and let some other guy take her off my hands. But I'd hate to try to spend another fifty-three years training another one to fry my bacon just right.

You guys enjoy the West Virginia sunshine and think once in a while about us old incompetents who are 'way up north freezing our _____ off. (You can fill in the blank space with one or more words of your own choosing).

I've got to run. I've got some books to sign and some fish to catch.

Love to y'all,
Margy and Bill

My Daddy Was a Truck Drivin' Man
and I Feel Like I Have Been on a Couple of Long Trips Myself

My father was a man of varied experience. And that was just in the workplace. I'm not telling about the other places.

One of his careers near the end of his brief but flamboyant life was driving a rig for B&L Truck Lines out of Newark, Ohio. He was pulling double bottoms before most of us learned what to do with only one.

His life was snuffed out when he came around a curve near Lowell, Ohio and swerved his Coupe de Ville off the left side of the road to avoid a farm tractor going the same way he was and several miles per hour slower. An oncoming truck swerved to the same flat spot and parked its front wheel in the rear seat of the Caddy. The path of travel took it over the steering wheel.

I don't know what ever happened to old B&L. I haven't seen one of their logos for years. They may have gone the way of some of the other old-timers like Bell, Smith, Priority, and "The Handshakers," Mason and Dixon.

Trucking was once a hard way to make an easy living. Evolution has changed all that--with a little help from the state DOT's, PSC's, PUC's, and the granddaddy of them all, the Federal ICC.

Truck drivers today are all as rich as Croesus and drive Lincolns and El Dorados which Croesus could never afford. If you don't believe me, ask any owner-operator how easily he makes the payments on his rig and how he manages to maintain it in tip-top shape.

Truck drivers today are only somewhat similar to their ancestral counterparts of only a few years back. All with loads that are too heavy, engines that are too weak, and gear boxes with as many as twenty-one shifts or more to get them up one hillside and down the other. Especially if they don't have a "Jake Brake." Gearing down going down can be trickier than gearing down going up.

They still live on greasy hamburgers, greasy French Fries, a dash of ketchup to alter the taste, and lots of coffee with an oily scum on top. The real veterans have substituted Tabasco for the ketchup in order to put a little spice in their lives.

If you have a tendency to cast a bleary eye the other way at some of the didoes our government is cutting, you had better quit dozing in front of the set and pay attention before they start chipping away at your civil rights. You have probably lost a few already, but were to drowsy to notice. Truck drivers just lost another.

I just read that the Congress has made it illegal to use a radar detector in a vehicle used in interstate commerce. I'll bet that will grab truck drivers where the hair is short and where the allotted time to run from Sugar City to The Windy is even shorter, or if one is running a load of fresh vegetables which have a time problem from Shakyside to the Big Apple.

"Lemon Squeezers" have it made. They run from Motor City to deliver their loads to every car dealer this side of Japan. They never have to hurry to meet a schedule, are never overloaded, and their "car-goes" are getting smaller all the time so they can haul more of them without raising a DOT officer's eyebrows. If they remembered to get the proper permits of passage.

Another way that evolution has improved truck drivers is that their spare tires are getting bigger and better. And there are more of them. Most single rigs have something close to eighteen on the pavement. I have tried to count the tires on some of the singles in that country north of Niagara Falls. I ran out of fingers three times and gave up.

Truck tires rarely blow out nowadays except when you are on the Big Road and running two hours or more behind schedule with a "hot" load and the shoulders are soft

Any number of things can happen in that case, like the tread peeling from a carcass, leaving the alligator in the fast lane for the next guy to run over. That event is sometimes repeated because of the extra load on the tire's cellmates. It is most likely to happen on isolated stretches where you are forty miles from fixers.

Truck drivers themselves are a different breed today, but only slightly. Evolution has given them CB radios which they use constantly to tell each other how much weight they are pulling and what size their too-small engines are, where all the "Smokeys" are hiding with their picture takers, where the diners with the friendliest waitresses are, and where they can get an over-priced cup of coffee. They might even talk about the high price of diesel or where the handiest truck stop is located.

In the old days, they had to find out all those things for themselves.

Truck drivers have made one tremendous change. Power steering doesn't require the brute strength that the earlier gear-type did. As a result of that and some other mechanical improvements, the once-male field has been infiltrated by females. I have seen some of those who were definitely a physical improvement over the old type, and my eyes aren't what they used to be.

If the scenery continues to get better, I just might quit writing and go into some other line of work.

I would have already if I didn't have to put up with drivers of "four-wheelers" just like me who follow a big rig driver about three feet behind his bumper so if anyone gets photographed on radar, it will be him who forgot to say "Cheese." Or who pass him while he is cruising along at eighty and slam on the brakes so that his trailer starts running down the freeway crossways. That curdles his coffee that is now running all over the floorboards. Or who buzz around him while he is huffing and puffing diesel smoke trying to get a run for White Oak Mountain without needing a push and then slow down so he loses his speed just before he hits the slope. That'll grab his Granny.

Interest in Interest Rates

I bounced out of bed this morning after only ten or twelve hours sleep, rushed into the den and collapsed in my recliner to watch the news on television. And that was before breakfast. I make all those sacrifices for you so you won't lose your beauty sleep.

There almost as big as one-sixth life (I have a small screen) was Stewart Varney interviewing some guy about interest rates.

I could hardly believe my ears when Stew started asking some of the same questions which I have been asking ever since that other guy, Shrub or something like that, was in that big Outhouse in Washington and beating the bushes for lower interest rates.

What was even more amazing was that Stew either caught him completely off-guard or his mind was a little numble (mine gets that way, too) and he blurted out the truth before he knew what he was saying. He grabbed an old dustrag and started drying his shoes, both of which were covered with moisture from foot-in-mouth disease. He was too late. I had already heard him.

He said that the Wall Street moneychangers were the ones who were making all the money on the lowered rates. When the rates crept up like old long johns, the money-grubbers started losing their collective shirts. It seems they weren't born salesmen and were having all kinds of trouble peddling yesterday's papers. They had picked up the then-lucrative papers at bargain basement prices, hoping to make a killing by selling them to unsuspecting suckers. The cut-throats' knife slipped and pointed directly at theirs. They bleed green.

I tried to tell Americans nationwide in all the major papers which would print my article what was happening when George and Alan got their noggins together and gave the big shove that started rates on their bob-sled ride. I saw only two major papers that carried the article, The Bluefield Daily Telegraph and The Ritchie Gazette. I don't know about the others, but I did hear about a few more that are rather well-known.

Soon after I wrote the article, I saw a couple on television (Where else?) who had just stumbled on to a real bargain. They paid $212,000 for a house with a seven percent mortgage which had been advertised two months before for $162,500 at eight and one-half percent. Excuse me for a couple of minutes while I hunt for my solar-powered calculator.

The interest savings for the first year was $1,028. The guy who saved it was the mortgagor. The builder was grinning all the way to the bank with his little windfall.

You must remember that took place in one of those suburbs of one of our larger villages. It couldn't happen in our neck of the woods.

Today, the venerated and venerable, vacillatory. vilifying, vituperative, vindicatory, vaporous varlet who is the vassal of the President and Sec'y of the Treasury was trying to eliminate the small gains in interest rates upon which some of us old hillbillies depend upon for the bread and butter which goes with our ramps and brown beans.

It makes me wonder if he is vested as a vendor or a vendee in a few vendable papers.

Postscript:

I once made up an old saw that went, "Put a little aside for your old age. It happens a lot sooner than you can imagine."

Alan and George, with a little cheering from the rooting section, managed to push interest rates on some bank accounts down to as low as under three percent. If you paid income taxes on your interest income, you were only losing about one or two percent per year.

They, along with higher medical costs and lower Medicare payments; loss of hair, hearing, sight, and teeth; loss of another thing or two; higher utility bills; more real estate taxes; etc., have made it hardly worthwhile to grow old.

Spies and Counter-Spies

The television news channels and some of the national network news programs have recently been swamped with the "news" that Russia is still spying on us as evidenced by the uncovering of an undercover agent who was also a top dog in our own CIA.

Shame on them!

It came out from somewhere out in the cold that we were paying him to do Russia's dirty work. Indirectly, of course. He and his wife got a measly two million (other reports said one and a half million, but who wants to quibble over a little thing like that) of the billions we have sent to Russia for financing of such projects. No wonder the trade deficit is so out of whack. They probably sent the rest of it to China and Iraq.

If you know anything at all about the business, you have already read some of the jargon used when spies, counter-spies, superspies, and just plain Joes and Janes get together to talk shop. I don't know who let the cat out of the closet and slipped a few codewords to the media, but we are having a field day with them. They make us sound to the unwashed as though we know what we are talking about.

The word "mole" may have been among the first to shed the shackles. We have been using it with a professional ring that causes the laity to sit up and take notice. I don't understand why.

A mole (without " ") is a small, fuzzy, nearly-blind,

145

burrowing animal that eats bugs and rips your backyard to shreds while searching for Junebug embryoes in your bluegrass. He doesn't have enough sense to run around on top of the ground where there is more light and bug-hunting would be easier and more profitable. You never see a robin digging mile-long holes to get something to eat.

A "mole" (with " ") is a small, fuzzy, nearly-blind animal which burrows into the "enemy" spy network, usually that of his own homeland, and performs a few simple tasks for the "enemy" like looking for bugs, rooting out secrets, etc. in order to get a few tidbits for his trainers, also called "handlers."

Every "mole" has one or more handlers. Those are higher class spies who slip the mole a few dollars for information he digs up. Much of the information is already known to the network. If he does happen to stumble on to something of value, that information is checked and double-checked to make certain the mole has not turned hindside foremost and started burrowing the other way. If "they" don't catch him turning tail, a mole can live in some pretty nice holes. If they do catch him with mud on his face, he gets a tailored-to-fit hole that is more or less a permanent abode. No marker.

That is over there. Over here, we give him a nice room with a full bath and a view, a TV so he can watch the evening news, plenty of reading material containing top secrets, catered meals, and in-room visitation privileges from any of his favorite girl-friends.

There are other words that we media people use to fool the public into thinking that we are smarter than the run-of-the-bar cocktail swiller. Two of those words are "covert" and its antithesis "overt." Some of us use big words instead of small ones to keep you guessing.

"Covert" is just another way of saying "under-cover." I haven't met a newsman or a television commentator yet (males only) who did not think he was better than any of his contemporaries at that job. The attitude has rubbed off on to some of the common people of the same species, particularly salesmen.

I have been too busy to interview the opposite sex, so I have no idea what they think. I very likely wouldn't know if I had devoted my entire seventy-two years to such research.

"Overt" is just the opposite of "covert." It simply means that you don't care who knows what you do nor if they see you doing it. It is becoming more prevalent in our society, especially the kind of society you see on television.

Spies and other government personnel often use code names for their projects. One recent example was "Tailhook." Everybody knows what a tailhook is. It is that little hangy-down thing with a hook on the end that hangs down from the belly of the plane. When a pilot makes a landing on a "flattop" the hook catches something or another and stops him in his tracks so he won't fall off the other end and make an ass of himself. I have no idea why they named that dirty little party

"Tailhook." One has no relationship to the other unless the pilots were afraid of falling off something.

We just heard another new one, "Lightning Strike." It netted a few suckers in NASA. I don't know if the name meant that it would never be done again. It may have been a signal to clear the way for more shenanigans, since lightning is said to never strike twice in the same place.

Spies have code names, too. One of the most famous of recent spies was called "Intrepid." At least one other was called "Chicken," but that may not have been his code name. A few have only a single letter. Like "Q". If I didn't know better, I would likely think a spy who only rated a single letter didn't amount to a whole lot.

Now you know everything you need to start kindergarten in your favorite spy school. A good one shouldn't be too hard to find. Every country has at least one. Several countries have more than one right here. You may not have to leave home to make money hand over fist.

Just be sure to pick a country we have been financing. They have the most money. And it isn't counterfeit.

And think up a good code name.

National Biological Survey (Boondoggle)

You wouldn't believe some of the things that go on on television, especially if you watch Congress in inaction on C-Span.

I've been at it again! Watching my favorite comedy channel, the one that shows Congress enacting one crazy bill after another. If you haven't been watching, you need to know what Congress is now trying to do while you aren't looking.

They are now considering the authorization of a new boondoggle called The National Biological Survey. I had a good deal of trouble trying to determine the real purpose of the project. It didn't take much time at all to figure what the underestimate of the cost is.

The price tag which Congress stuck on this piece of nonsense is $180,000,000 (that's right, one-hundred-eighty-million). I'll bet that will grab you where it hurts. Just wait until you learn what Congress proposes to do with all that borrowed cash. When you get out your calculator to compute the cost and the overrun, don't forget to include the interest.

I talked with Jay Rockefeller several months ago about the artificially reduced interest rates. He said that lower rates were necessary to HELP REDUCE THE DEFICIT. And you thought all the time that it was supposed to be done with spending cuts.

That burden falls mostly on us old people who mistakenly thought that we should work hard, spend less than we brought home, lay a little aside for our dotage, and help support politicians and other people who were apparently much smarter than us.

Congress is now considering spending a little of that Budget Reduction Money for what must seem to that bunch to be a worthwhile project. That money is to fund a census of all animals, plants, mushrooms, toadstools, algae, and other wildlife all over these United States. If you think that piddlin' amount will cover the cost, I have about eight thousand feet of waterfront property that I would like to talk about with you, provided you can get government backing.

I have read recently that waterfront property is going for as much as one-hundred-thousand dollars per square foot. My property lies along both sides of a ditch that a short-legged woman can step across. The stream once held crawdads, daces, bittergut minnows, chubs, stonefly nymphs, horny heads, tadpoles, hellgrammites, and other aquatic life. Cattle drank from it. Hogs waded belly deep in it to cool their lard.

Mine drainage from a settling pond seeped into it and now the hogs won't go near it, cows won't drink from it, and you couldn't find a specimen of wildlife in it if your life depended upon it. And everything was done according to law.

I can tell Congress how to save most of that money. Send out questionnaires to every landowner asking them what plants and animals grow on their property. That wouldn't cost anything for postage because they could include the form with the junk mail they already send out under the franking privilege.

The responses might contain some funny names, but they might be as accurate as the ones coined by the "experts." I heard of one water plant which was called three different things by three biologists. None of them knew what it was. I'll bet that half of them wouldn't know a hoary puccoon root from ginseng. If they did happen to recognize it, I'll bet they wouldn't know what to do with them. I'm not talking about the real biologists, just the government issue kind.

What happens if they do locate a left-lobed butter-bean plant isolated in some farmer's hundred acres of corn? If history is a reliable indicator of an ecologist's future reaction, we will sacrifice the cornfield for the rare specimen, which may never reproduce, since it is obviously a hybrid.

I am a conservationist. I believe in the wise and conservative use of our natural resources. I believe we should not waste them. I also believe that man is a part of the environment. Any environmental philosophy which does not recognize that fact and fails to include man in the equation is doomed to failure. I believe that extinction is a natural process. We do not need to hasten it, but neither do we need to perpetuate a species that is already past its time.

Man will one day become extinct. That is the species that deserves the most protection now. As the eternal clock ticks, our extinction may not be very far down the road. Let's not push it.

The hidden purpose of the National Biological Survey is to find RARE plants, animals, and insects. That might not be the stated purpose, but I can solid guarantee that is what will happen. The final analysis may show them to be neither rare nor endangered, but we will be told they are and that they are just as essential to our survival as the bison was to the Indians a few years ago.

If you remember what happened to the logging industry in our Pacific Northwest a few months back because of misinformation on the spotted owl, think what could happen to agriculture, timbering, oil and gas, coal mining, commercial fishing and crabbing, and any other extractive industry on a nationwide basis if someone happens to find a cross-eyed field mouse or a mock turtle. Remember the snail darter?

It would be a different story if we could believe what the scientists tell us. Some of them have fed us so many wild-eyed tales that not many of us common people know what to believe. Most of us hear with only one ear when they do tell us the truth.

I believe that we should protect species everywhere possible, but when one or the other must go, I will vote for man to survive every time. We will disappear from this big anthill soon enough. When that happens, the exotic cockroaches can set up housekeeping in all the domiciles we leave.

Meanwhile, let's try to keep our heads on straight.

Another Ramp Season Is Upon Us

The Great-Grandpappy of all West Virginia Ramp Festivals will be held in Richwood on April 16 this year.

People go there by the hundreds to load up on brown beans, fried potatoes, fried ham, corn bread, dessert, and the piece de resistance, the lowly little wild leek that us lowly hillbillies call ramps. The elite among us call it ramson.

You can change the spelling, but there ain't a whole awful lot you can do about the smell. A ramp by any other name smells just as bad. There ain't much you can do about the smell of ramp-eaters, either.

About 99.8% of the people who attend the festival load up on something else. That is the fun and frolic and camaraderie of good country people and good city slickers who were once good country people or wish they had been. The other .2% cook the ramps, fry the ham and taters, wait on tables, do all the planning and the leg-work and wind up having more fun than anyone else and more than twice the frolic. They spend more time at it.

What with one thing and another, my digging the little rascals has gone unattended for nigh on to three months now. My eating has suffered exponentially.

Any of my readers who have been paying attention to Jim Comstock over the past few years know that I have a smelly reputation for purloining a pocketful or two of the pew-ful peewee-size bulbs somewhat early--

usually just before Christmas or right after New Year.

By the time the tops pop through the topsoil, I have normally had eight or ten tender messes. That is when most people start their reaping of the ramson. That is just about the time I stop.

I will snatch a few tender tops on occasion to toss into my tossed salad. The secret to "top-notch" salad is in the ratio of ramps to radishes. Too much of either or any of the other components and the salad isn't salad any more.

The global warming we experienced in these parts and in parts of Canada in January and February of this year messed up our ramp digging. The heat froze everything solid, including the thick layer of ice on top of the thick layer of snow. When Canada's warm spell turned into their coldest on record, they shipped the excess minus readings down through the hills of Appalachia (wherever that is) and messed up our weather, our travel, and my ramp patch. We managed to get the four-wheel drive to the parking place, but my wife and I couldn't stand up on the ice.

I was beginning to think that the next ice age was just around both corners--the one we just turned and the one we are about to turneth.

I saw the sunshine the other day, so if you sneak into the woods behind us, you may see my wife and I scratching for ramps. We will be behind the wild turkeys who normally scratch out a few a day or so before we get there. She will be the one carrying the big bucket.

See you at the Feast of the Ramson. I'll be the big old ugly guy sitting behind the desk selling my funny book. We might even swap a story or two.

The following recipes were not included in the original article. I thought you might like to know how one old hillbilly fixes ramps. You might want to know if they are really as good as the connoisseurs claim.

When I fix ramps, I fix a frying pan full. It takes that many for my wife and I to feel fullish. If you want less, adjust the recipe, but don't cut down too much on the last ingredient.

Dig and clean enough ramps to fill a 10-inch frying pan rounded full. Just the stems, mind you. If you like the leaves, you had better fix them your own way.

Cut one pound of sliced lean bacon into one-inch pieces. Fry until almost done. Remove bacon from skillet and place in dish at side. You will use it later.

Add about 12 ounces of water to bacon grease. Add the ramps until heaped. Cover and allow to cook slowly until ramps become somewhat clear. Remove cover and continue to cook until water is gone. Add about one cup of white cooking wine (I prefer Vermouth). Cover again and allow to simmer for about three minutes. Remove cover and allow liquid to evaporate. Add the pieces of bacon which you set aside. Continue frying until ramps begin to turn brown.

155

You will need to stir frequently during the entire process. I prefer a wooden spatula.

Serve with T-Bone steak, baked potato, salad, and skip the dessert.

Most of us eat them with corn bread, brown beans cooked with ham, and a little ham on the side. They are delicious regardless of what you want for a side dish.

My wife fixes the larger stems by French Frying. Parboil the ramps until nearly done. Remove from water and drain on three or four layers of paper towels. This usually takes about an hour. Ramps must be thoroughly dry.

Mix a thick batter made from complete pancake mix. Heat a pan of oil to the point that a drop of batter begins to cook immediately. Dip each ramp individually in the batter until fully coated, then drop it into the hot oil. Don't overcrowd the skillet. Fry until golden brown. Serve as hot as possible.

Fix plenty. When we eat them that way, we rarely eat anything else with them. After the first snitched ramp, you may want to eat them as they come out of the skillet.

Enjoy the eating.

Me and Juanita and Ramps and the United States Postal Service

I know it isn't ramp season yet, but I decided that it was about time for me to tantalize your taste buds with a few memories of the little delights. You might get your funnybone tickled at the same time.

I have a pair of long-time friends. They are Jack and Juanita Messenger of Union Deposit, Pa., almost a suburb of Chocolate City.

They are the completely opposite of me in shifting states. I was just barely born in Pennsylvania and moved to West Virginia to find fame and fortune. They were born in West Virginia and moved to Hershey to become house parents to a houseful of Mr. Hershey's proteges. Jack was also the manager of the dairy farm. He had been a farmer in the head of a holler between Morgantown and Fairmont.

Juanita was reared on ramps. I knew her parents as friends and neighbors. God richly blessed me with their friendship. They may have used a ramp or two instead of a pacifier when Juanita was just a little thing. She never got over her addiction to them. She will eat every one she lays eyes on. It makes no difference if they are raw, fried, steamed, or fixed some other way.

I'm not sure about Jack. He may have had to eat them in self-defense.

I have only a few heroes. You can almost count them on the hand of one finger. Jim Comstock has been

157

one of them for many years.

Jim has his faults, but so does any other hero. One of his faults is a long-time love affair with a siren of the hills, the lowly little ramp.

He even went so far one time as to salt his ink with ramp juice. The Post Office gave him a reprimand for raising such a big stink. They let him off easy with the solemn promise with his right hand raised and his left on a pile of old copies of his paper, The West Virginia Hillbilly, that he would never do it again. If I remember correctly, they reinforced the promise with a restraining order, but don't quote me.

Luckily, it wasn't worse. Anyone who would print a newspaper with ramp juice ought to be condemned to eating all of them he can beg, borrow, dig, scrounge, and steal until he is at least a hundred and ten. He ought not be compelled to eat more than his slim frame can hold without splitting at the seams. They should be properly prepared, of course.

I try to emulate Jim--up to a point.

I felt sorry for Juanita and Jack, living up there where everything smells like one big chocolate bar. And not a single ramp to break the monotony. You can't inhale deeply up there more than three times a day without gaining two pounds. The street lights are even shaped like Hershey kisses.

You all know that I am an early digger. I normally start to dig as soon as the ground is frozen to a depth of three or four inches.

I decided that I could ship the little stinkers before they started to shoot up their shoots. I dug a mess and washed off all the good mountain dirt. I didn't want to export any of that to someplace where it might become polluted with all that organic fertilizer they keep piled behind the barns. If you get a ways out of town to where the Jerseys and the Charolais play, the aroma overcomes the odor of the city, especially when the spreaders are hard at it.

I packed the ramps in Zip-Loks three thick. You know the kind they advertise on TV as being stink-proof. I wanted to use the very best. I didn't dare take any chances with escaped vapors.

I then shipped them by Priority Mail which was guaranteed to get them there in two days. I sent several packages over a two-spring period with the Post Office being none the wiser. I suppose I got over-confident.

I am a firm believer in Berdine's Law which goes Murphy one better. I have said for years that if anything can't possibly go wrong, it will anyhow.

Juanita remembered the delicate flavor of ramp leaves. She wanted some. She had tried planting a few in her flower pots, but the chipmunks and squirrels up there learned they were good to eat and gobbled them up faster than she could tote them out and dig the holes.

Being the un-genius that I am, I agreed after only the feeblest of protests to find a way. I explained to her that we might run into problems, but I have always been a push-over when a woman starts to cry.

159

I would ship a few which were just beginning to come into their own with only the tips of the leaves showing. I packed those in four layers of Zip-Loks to the package and then sealed the whole kit and caboodle in plastic. Any of you who know ramps will know why.

When they start to grow, they emit a powerful gas-- and I don't mean just for odor. They will melt snow, just like skunk cabbage and other plants.

As bad luck would have it, my priority mail lost its capital letters. It got itself kicked into the corner of the Hershey Post Office for the weekend. I had marked the package in big black letters, "Do not store near heat."

Guess where it landed. The gas unzipped the Zip-Loks from the inside and burped its way into the post office. It didn't smell like a chocolate bar. Zip-Lok would have hidden their heads under their wings.

Juanita looked out her kitchen window early Monday morning and saw a U.S. male driver in a U.S. mail truck in the alley where none had ever been. He bounced out of the truck and trotted toward the back door empty-handed.

When she went out, there was her mail-order surprise package tied to the rear bumper of the otherwise empty truck.

It took her nearly thirty minutes of fast talking to clear my name and my tarnished reputation. He was sure I had shipped her a putrid pussycat. She explained that I had already shipped about twenty or thirty packages of ramps without raising a stink.

He said, "Shipped what?" She tried to explain ramps, but there are some things for which you just can't find enough words to explain to a flatlander. The clincher came when she invited him into the kitchen to watch her open the box. He politely said that he would just as soon wait outside. Harry Truman became famous with the media for saying, "If you can't stand the heat, get out of the kitchen." after he heard his Grandma say it. The postal worker's reluctance to step inside had nothing to do with temperature unless you want to count the earlier misapplied heat. He couldn't stand the smell.

He peeked through the window while she finished the unpacking which the ramps had started. She pulled one from the package, cleaned it and handed it to him through the half-opened door. He sniffed and curled his lip. Then he said, "Oh, what the ------." He popped the pew-ful little thing into his mouth in imitation of Juanita and munched. Then he stepped into the kitchen and proceeded to finish nearly half a package. Raw!

I got off the hook, but I'll bet that when he returned to the post office, he was the one who had to stand in the corner.

Out in the corner of the cow pasture where the spreaders were just finishing their chores.

My Incredible Incurable Addiction

I realize that all of my readers believe that I am just a little more than perfect, but I must admit that I do have one little fault. I suppose that you could just call it a bad habit if you feel like being kind.

I drink coffee! I am a chain-cup caffeine addict. Other people have simple problems like cigarettes or beer. Neither of those easy-to-kick habits has ever bothered me in the least, but you just try kicking the coffee habit.

I have been drinking four and more quarts every day for more years than I can remember. That's right-- QUARTS.

Almost every doctor I visited for some real or imagined ailment told me that I must quit. I suppose they thought that too much of a good thing might adversely affect the amount of available time during which I could partake of all the other good things to which I am only somewhat addicted.

I searched for more than fifty years and consulted dozens of doctors while trying to find one with a little common sense. I finally found one after the others had given me up as moribund.

He examined me all over, using the most modern equipment which was available forty years before he was born. He said I was in perfect health. I began to feel better all over until he added, "For your age." Then he verified his original diagnosis on his more ex-

expensive equipment. Two hours and more than five hundred dollars later, he confirmed his first findings. That was fourteen years ago.

He told me to start drinking a gallon of water a day. When I protested that there was no way that I could hold a gallon of water, he responded, "Anybody can hold a gallon of water. And start eating lots of onions."

I asked, "How about ramps?" "Oh, yeah! Ramps are better for you than onions, but eat all you can of both. Tell your wife to start drinking a gallon too."

It was about that time that I told him of my addiction. When I told him how much coffee I poured down my gullet, three and four mugs at a time, he erupted. He fairly shouted his response. "You're doing what?" When I iterated my statement with my right hand over my head and my left on my U.S. belt buckle, he nearly fell over in a dead faint. When he recovered, he was still insisting on the gallon of water a day. I asked him a simple question. "Where in tarnation do you expect me to put it. On top of all that coffee?"

Then I explained how we made our coffee.

We are inherently close with our few paltry pieces of filthy lucre. I have been accused of selling buffalo hides on several occasions. I learned years ago that coffee beans, crushed or whole, furnish fine foci for frugality.

If you have visited your corner grocery lately, you are already suffering from frostbite of the little red bean that cooks up brown and makes a delightful broth when

163

boiled. The cans shrunk by nine ounces a few years ago and now the price has lunged into the luxury class.

When I told that young man who is now my old country doctor that we made twelve cups at a time in our automatic drip using one tablespoon of ADC M.H., he slapped his thigh so hard it cracked and broke into uncontrollable laughter. "Drink all of it you want. It'll never hurt you."

Now that doctor has common sense. If you study the picture beside my byline, you can plainly see that it hasn't.

And I'm all of twenty-seven.

Un Bel Di

I have no idea why I titled this column with the name of the aria. It may be that "One Fine Day" most accurately describes a day spent in the woods with your .410 looking for squirrels or with your souped-up bow looking for deer.

I don't hunt any more. I haven't for several seasons now. I have developed a couple of things in fairly recent years besides old age that slow me down a mite.

I haven't, for one thing, found a partner who is big enough to tote me back to the car. I suddenly developed a broken back 'way back there in '66. I sometimes fall flat and can't stand on my own two feet. That sort of takes the fun out of climbing a dozen feet or so to sit in my once-favorite perch.

One of the finest days I have spent hunting was a few years back, but I can remember it clearly. Maybe more than many others.

I spent a couple of days prior to the season building a stand in a clump of trees that were little more than oversized saplings. I carried 2x4's and a big piece of plywood to the site. I need a thick piece of plywood to keep me suspended in space, what with my 225 lbs. of solid fat and my accompanying accouterment. That includes but is not limited to at least three quart bottles of coffee, eight pounds or so of lunch and snacks, about seventy pounds of assorted necessities (most of which I have yet to use), and oh, yes, my bow and arrows.

I whacked off all the brush within shooting distance of the stand with my trusty machete. There were numerous scrapes and rubs, indicating the presence in the general area of a deer of the male gender. It looked as if he were a good one.

I had squatters rights on the property and the trees would never grow up to be anything more than scrubs, so I used my own unpatented in-tree steps for access to my tree-top boudoir. I reinforced the subfloor with four of the 2x4's on edge and laid the plywood on top. It was big enough to hold a jitterbug contest.

I am afraid of heights when my feet are both off the ground more than about a foot, so I make my stands big enough that if I fall I will land on something solid not too far below my ankles. I wear a safety belt anyway.

On opening day I bounced out of bed and limped all the way to the kitchen so I could rattle the coffee pot and other pans to wake my little half.

One of her assigned chores for the past fifty-odd years has been to fix me a hearty breakfast so I won't starve during the day. Why else would I take her along on all my hunting and fishing trips?

Breakfast used to be our largest meal of the day when I lived on the farm. I wrote somewhere earlier of all the things we ate for breakfast, so I won't go into that here. We fixed buckwheat cakes, graham cereal, homemade bread, sausage or bacon or some other kind of hog meat, home-squeezed milk, home-boiled coffee, and two or three other goodies to fill the spaces.

166

One of the things that comes up missing when you get too old to chew is your hearty appetite. Today I leave out the graham cereal, but I substitute instant oatmeal or cold cereal. I wouldn't want to cause some physical or medical calamity by quitting "cold turkey."

I packed my lunch while she was frying and fixin' my breakfast. You couldn't believe how much stuff you can stuff into one of those back packs. Four full-sized sandwiches, a dozen or so cookies, two candy bars (the 7 oz. size), two full sticks of pepperoni, three big apples, a couple of cold pork chops, and a few trail bars in case I get hungry.

I made sure my three Stanleys were full and hot. Then I started to get ready.

I donned my camo clothing, made sure I had both rain suits (in case I ripped one), and daubed camo paint all over my face and hands and on my other parts that might accidentally become bare for some reason or another.

I went to the back porch to pour the red fox pee all over my expensive new boots so the buck wouldn't know it was me and so the wood cook stove wouldn't warm my boots and cause a delay talking over the day's events before it had barely started.

You can't believe how long that stuff lasts and how it permeates the atmosphere when you bring your boots into the house and dry them by the stove. You can't believe how upset the female gender can get when they have to stay in the house after the boots have gone.

I was on my way at last. I bumped into no more than nineteen trees and bushes as I stumbled up the hill to my stand. I unloaded my gear, lashed it together with a rope, and pitched the loose end over the stand. I tied a smaller cord to my bow and pitched the cord across the stand beside the rope.

Then I poured a dab of female deer estrus extract in each of the scrapes. I have no idea how they get so much of that stuff. I'll bet somebody has to run like the very blazes while holding that little bottle. He must have a pretty steady hand. After all the trouble some-one had to go to, it should drive an eager buck absolutely wild.

I carefully pulled my gear and my armory up to the stand and hung them on the hooks I had installed for just such an occasion. I poured a cup of coffee and placed it on the little shelf which I had so thoughtfully provided. Then I sat to contemplate.

I was in my stand and settled a while before dawn cracked. I waited one candy bar, one sandwich, and one quart of coffee before I heard a slight rustle in some wild grape and greenbrier vines directly in front of my stand and too far away to shoot. If there is anything I know at all, it is my limitations with a bow.

A beautiful eight-pointer cautiously stepped into view and audibly inhaled. I don't know if it was the red fox pee or the estrus scent that made his eyes light up, but he threw caution to the breeze and trotted directly under the stand to one of the scrapes.

He was no more than ten yards away with his head pointed east. I was to the west.

I drew the sixty-five pound compound bow without a sound. I still don't know why he turned his head. It may have been a doe which caught his attention. Suddenly I was looking directly into his big brown eyes and he was looking directly into my watery blue ones.

I eased the tension off the bow just as he nodded, "Thanks. I shouldn't have been so anxious." I watched as he ambled to each doctored scrape and sniffed. I thought, "Oh, what the heck? Let him enjoy being duped." I didn't want to clean a bloomin' deer anyhow.

The sun was giving the gold, scarlet, purple, and brown leaves their morning kisses. Birds were beginning to warble their territorial songs. I could almost swear I could hear one of them whistling "Un Bel Di." He must have spent the evening at the opera.

I leaned back, opened another quart of coffee and just looked and listened.

It was truly "One Fine Day."

Especially for me and for the buck.

Dad's Pool Room

Grandpa Parry helped Dad get started in business in the hope that he could become self-supporting to some degree. The drain on Grandpa's financial resources was interfering with his retirement plan. The income simply wasn't in the same footrace with the outgo.

Dad found a real money-maker. The general merchandise retailer (otherwise known as a country store owner) who operated the poolroom on the side of his store had been trying to unload it for several years. That country-rube super salesman dumped it when he shed those tears while telling Dad how much he hated to part with it.

Dad operated it for upwards of three years. The money he made hand-over-fist barely kept us eating. It is a good thing that we had free rent and free gas and that Mom took in washings to help feed us. She later fed a family of seven on a ten dollar monthly allowance, so she knew how to manage.

And how to pick wild plants that gave us most of our green groceries, supplemented by a few cabbages, beans, and potatoes from her garden.

She even rented the spare room to the school teacher in the winter to help bring in an extra dollar or two from room and board. Female school teachers don't eat that much.

That teacher took me under her wing and tried to teach me what she could in the first grade.

She was also the one who taught me that using the kind of language which I learned down behind the barn was not an acceptable standard of conduct when talking with pretty little first-grade girls. She was emphatic. She stressed her point with a hickory switch that she kept on hand for such emergencies.

I am not sure that what Dad did could be called running a poolroom. It is a lead-pipe cinch that it didn't run him. He may have made more money than the earlier paragraph indicates, but if he did, it went for other commodities that wouldn't have dared show their faces at our back door. Mom would have crowned them with a broom or a mop.

The poolroom was located in a large village that boasted a population in the twenties. That was large compared to ours. It boasted all of nine residents. The village was a long seven miles of dirt road and a couple of steep slopes from our house.

Poolrooms back then stayed open just as long as potential customers had two nickels to click together. It was the job of the budding entrepreneur to detect the click and to separate the coins from the nickel-bearing ore. That often took until one or two o'clock in the morning on week days and somewhat later on Saturday when the dark window-blinds were pulled to keep nosy neighbors from watching. There were strict blue laws in that far-back area which were enacted and policed by the folks who could be sitting in the pews on Sunday, come deep snows or high water. They frowned on Sunday shenanigans that might or might not have included dirty pool. I have heard rumors or gossip that the poolroom was often busy without benefit of proprietor--sort of an honor system among hoodwinkers. I have also heard that it was the only poolroom in the state where women could shoot to their hearts' content. After hours and with the shades drawn.

The booming business boasted two tables and nearly ten times as many cue sticks. That used up all the available space except for the Coca Cola ice chest which sat in the corner waiting for someone who had an uncontrollable thirst and a nickel at the same time. I am not sure, but I do not believe that anything stronger than an overpowered coffee was sold there. As far as I know, Dad never lost any cue sticks through accidental collisions with bone, but some of them were a little warped near the middle.

There were times when the four pool sharks who hung around the premises either on the bench on the front porch or sprawled in most of the six metal chairs inside kept both tables going with promises of instant wealth to itinerant drummers, oil-rig builders (they used wood back then), drillers, horse traders, sheep-dippers, and other wayward wanderers. There were even times when there was a person or two waiting in line to part with a few nickels or dimes to help fill the sharks' desire for change. Dad worked on a percentage of the take from side bets plus the price of the game to cover the rent.

172

The side-bar bets rarely exceeded twenty-five cents. The point losses rarely exceeded one or two balls. Once in a blue moon, the suckers won a game of eight-ball. I am getting old and crotchety and a few things have slipped my mind, but I can't recall any patsy walking away with more money than he had when he tiptoed in. If one did, it must have been a rare case of miscalculation on the part of the hustler who liked to shoot the last ball.

I have never figured how a pool stick pusher could read his victims with such uncanny accuracy. I once thought that I was pretty good with a stick. I went to Waynesburg on some pretext or another and arrived a couple of hours before the time that I was supposed to meet her on her front porch. When you hitch-hiked back in those days you had to allow a lot more time for hiking than for hitching.

I stumbled into an upstairs poolroom. There was only one old man sitting over in one corner and looking as though he had lost his last friend in a shooting match. He must have been all of forty.

I decided I would shoot a single to pass the time. I put my dime on the counter, picked a long cue, and proceeded to pocket seven straight balls. I had only a few pesos to see us through a movie and a visit to the Waynesburg Dairy where they sold the best Peanut Butter ice cream on the continent. And the cones were BIG. I didn't dare waste much time nor money on such foolishness as pool, so I slowed to bouncing the balls off the bumpers to make my dime last as long as possible.

The lonesome stranger ambled over and suggested we shoot a game. He offered to pay.

I jumped on that offer like a goose on a June Bug. I won that game by a fair margin. He suggested that we play another, loser pays. I lost that one by a single ball. When he suggested that we make a little bet, I lit a shuck out of there before I lost my supper money.

He wept.

I never really understood the applied psychology of hustling until many years later when I had entered what must have been my seventeenth profession, selling. It was also my first in terms of loving my work. I am not lying to you when I say that there were many Sundays when I could hardly wait for Monday morning to roll around so I could get back on the road.

I was working with a fellow salesman one week. He was supposed to be pretty good with a stick, according to his own statements and beliefs. We visited a mine in southern West Virginia and, since it was nearing noon, we invited the purchasing agent to lunch.

That p.a. (also pool shark) was and still is a good friend of mine, but I never let him sweet-talk me into playing eight-ball with him. I had heard stories about his ineptness at shooting pool from some of his fellow workers and from some who had listened to the soft soap that cleansed their bill-folds and ended in their going home with their bare shoulders hanging out and a dozen or two big lies to tell their other halves.

174

That salesman was a good friend of mine, too. When the p.a. (alias p.s.) accepted our invitation and just happened to know of a little place down at the forks of the road, I didn't dare interfere too much. I did tell the salesman not to go green-eyed-greedy when he saw the green felt surface of a peculiar table which I had seen there on previous occasions. It looked a lot like the ones Dad had, but the price had gone up and the table collected the quarter before you could retrieve a single ball. You anted up your quarter, racked your own balls, and paid off your own gambling debts. I told him that I wasn't lending him any of my money to pay his. I had enough trouble staying one jump ahead of the bill collectors as it was.

It is hard to tell a story like this without mentioning names and I don't want the whole world and half of New Jersey to know about either of them. When they read this story, they will know who the principals are. That should be enough.

We ordered sandwiches and before the waitress could pour the coffee, the invitation was out and accepted. After at least ten seconds of haggling over bet size, they agreed on a dollar a game. That was exactly what the p.a. (a.k.a. p.s.) had planned from two weeks before we hit the door to his office.

I sat and shuddered. I could remember from somewhere in my past a guy who had the same kind of look.

The salesman should have become a bit suspicious when the p.a. ducked around the corner of the counter and pulled out a long skinny case covered with alligator fur, the original use of which must have been to cover something at least as long, bigger in diameter, and with sharp teeth. One piece alligator skins stretched over a metal frame that isn't an exact fit don't grow on bushes.

The p.a. (now p.s.) carefully extracted a two-piece stick. The upper end was embellished with a shiny yellow metal that retails for about four hundred frog-skins per ounce. There must have been at least eight ounces on the end, the ferrules, and just ahead of the leather grip. The long part was gussied up with ash, hickory, sapele, ebony, holly, and purpleheart inlays. Those woods may grow on trees but they don't become cheap cue sticks without some expensive hand labor.

The salesman chose a stick from the community rack, rolled it three or four times across the table to check its true, chalked the tip, and waded feet first into his get-rich-quick scheme.

If I hadn't put in my two-cents worth while we were riding down there in the car and insisted that he limit his losses, we could have had a fifty mile walk home and over two steep mountains where those rattle-tailed snakes come to roost.

As I recall, the salesman broke the first rack. He lost by only one ball which rather miraculously appeared just to one side of the p.a.'s last one. He lost only a dollar plus the table takes, but he made the mistake of flashing his opened wallet right where the fast eye of the p.s. could count the change.

He stepped over to my side and whispered, "I can take this guy." I came right back as quick as a flash with a smart answer, "Yeah."

The p.s. broke the second rack and missed an easy shot after he had run five balls straight. If you can guess by how much he won the second game, you get to rack the balls on your next outing. The salesman sidled over to me and whispered, "I can take this guy. I'm going to up the ante to five dollars and get my money back." When I removed my hands from his throat so that he could talk, he had already nodded agreement to only one more dollar game.

The salesman broke the third rack and made an astonishing two-ball run without scratching. Only about half of them belonged to the p.s. When the bets were picked up at the end of the game, the p.s. (a.k.a. p.a.) was only two sandwiches, a cup of coffee, two cans of Coke, and the salesman's money ahead. I was digging for my wallet to see if I had enough to buy lunch for all three.

When we got back into our car, my sales partner confided, "I wish you hadn't insisted on leaving so soon. I know I can beat him." I sincerely believe that he could have. If someone had swiped that fancy cue stick and made the p.a. shoot with a broken beer bottle.

The feeling that an amateur can consistently outplay a pro is obviously an overwhelming emotion that must be something akin to a man's belief that he is a better

177

lover than Casanova. Everyone of my acquaintance shares both opinions. It must not be something new. It must have been prevalent in that remote billiards parlor that was one narrow back room of a country store.

The drummers, riggers, drillers, and wanderers were generally good losers. They had to be. Dad kept a thirty-eight handy just in case some high-roller lost next month's rent money a dribble here and a drab there and couldn't come up with a convincing lie for his other half. That is the trouble with low stakes. The white money adds up to green before you know what happened to your fuzzy calculator.

The riggers and drillers were probably the least problem. They were rough and tumble brawlers when they decided to fight among themselves or with out-siders. When they lost at the tables, they were careful to have a little nest egg salted away under a board at the well-site which the hustlers couldn't pry loose. They laughed and slapped each other on the back and went back to setting crown pulleys, bull wheels, and every-thing in between and on both sides and above and below to get the wells up and running the Texas Tea from Pennsylvania.

They liked the kid who ran the poolroom. Dad was the father of one boy and almost a second before he was old enough to vote. He was known all over the place as a womanizer. He wasn't choosy about whether they had a license or not. The thirty-eight may have been a dual purpose back-up piece in case a husband came by.

Dad had installed a comfortable cot in the small side room. It was allegedly used for sleeping. The poolroom already looked like a huge jail cell the first time I saw it. Someone, maybe Dad, had installed iron bars at the windows. Those may have been dual-purpose, too, the least of which may have been to keep the sore losers from trying to recover their losses through illegal but maybe justifiable means. The loot was supposed to flow only in one direction.

I don't know if Dad actually entertained any female clients in the side room. I can't believe that he would have been that foolish. Women who played pool (or ball) in those days were the victims of a lot of looking-down-the-nose glares from the women who didn't or who hadn't been found out or thought they hadn't.

He did his best work in the master bedroom while the husband was absent on some contrived errand or on some month-long job to earn enough to keep him and his body, soul, and unfaithful wife together. I have been told that the procedure has now become a "new" standard.

I suppose that it may sound redundant, but Dad didn't spend many nights at home. He liked to hit the hot sauce once in a while, but he was not addicted to it. He puffed a cigarette every now and again. Those added up to a pack or two a day, if your calculator will convert hand-rolleds to tailor-mades. He was addicted to smoke. He liked women and women apparently liked him. They were both addicted to that habit.

179

I have no idea how many "lady friends" he had during the time he had the poolroom. The legendary reliable sources indicated that there were more than quite a few. He did manage to impregnate Mom between times. She gave birth to my brother, Ray, some time after the happy union had begun to show serious signs of deteriorating.

The reliable sources reported that he began to get a little nervous when his new used girl friend gave birth to a little brown-haired daughter. The girl friend happened to be the wife of a man who spent only one weekend a month at home. The rest of his life was spent some sixty miles north in a slave-labor camp which was also called a steel mill.

The situation might not have been so touchy if the girl's complexion had been different. The family was blonde. When the husband began to look for a brunette in either family, he had no success.

When the husband left his job and moved back home to be with his family and began carrying his shotgun to the general store and casting doubting eyeballs on the customers, talking to the rural mail carrier, and gabbing with the bi-weekly fish peddler, people began to whisper.

He soon determined for himself that the fish peddler was too old, the mail carrier too busy, and the male customers too infrequent. When he casually ambled the seven miles to Grandpa Parry's one weekend and asked for permission to hunt where there weren't any woods,

180

Dad disappeared out the back door and quickly put the big barn between himself and the house. He did sneak back that evening after dark to throw the rest of his clothes into a burlap bag. He didn't wait long enough to tell us kids "Goodbye."

He sold his poolroom that had required frequent subsidizing from a congress named Grandpa Parry. He unloaded it "in absentia" to a friendly native for about a third of what he had invested, stuck the cash in his jeans, stuck Grandpa P. for the balance, and struck out for parts ---------.

He may not have been the cause of the former delicate condition of his cohort, but his actions have caused me to declare in full faith in my father and in his amazing abilities that somewhere in this old country there is a half-sister that must look a lot like me. She probably has more hair.

When he took off at a fast trot, he never looked back to see who was gaining. The next time we heard from him, he was in Panama, shooting pythons with his .45 Army pistol and petting pulchritudinous Panamanians.

The second activity put him in the Army hospital, but that story will have to wait until I see you again.

I hear my wife calling to tell me lunch is ready.

A True Short Story

I hinted in the preceding story that I learned to speak mule-skinnerese at a tender age. I quit at an age that was almost as tender. There were parts of my anatomy that had become tender from all the poundings with willow or hickory. This event took place between the ends of my addiction to lye soap.

My Granddad Berdine was a strict Baptist. He didn't use foul words and frowned on any of his children or further descendants when they slipped. He was also a fisherman, just like me.

He and the Reverend from his church took me to the North Fork of Hughes River to teach the preacher how it was supposed to be done. I was just over ten and a genuine expert. Granddad spotted a swirl just above the riffle and immediately delegated me to teach.

I showed the preacher how to hold the rod and how to thumb the reel. I also pointed out a likely looking spot at the end of a log. He tried, but you know how preachers are when it comes to fishing.

I took the rod, flipped the plug into the pocket and was into a fine bass. A BIG one. I went berserk, I guess. I bellowed at the top of my voice which was in fine fettle, "----- ------, Granddad! I got one!"

Granddad turned red all the way under his hat, the preacher fell to the rocks on the dry riffle and roared, and I put both hands over my face and ran for the truck. After I had landed the fish.

The High Cost of Vote Buying

Now that the other shoe has dropped and something like half of the candidates across the nation are dancing in the streets and nearly fifty percent are kicking the dog and the bedroom furniture, we will start totting up the costs of the campaigns.

There was once an old saying, "When you dance, someone must pay the piper." After all of us Scots, Irish, Scotch-Irish, English, Spanish, French, Polish, Italians, and a few other ethnic-come-latelies settled on all the good tobacco land, we became addicted to mountain music and started listening to banjer pickin' and fiddle playin'. Hardly anyone except for a few hardy souls from up there in Hardy County where they still tilt at iron rings and throw sawlogs barehanded remember the bagpipe squeezer. We changed the saying to "Pay the fiddler."

It still means that when you play at politicin', somebody has to hock his boots to foot the bill for all the newly-elected officials and all the oldly unelected un-officials.

It may, like the gentle rain from heaven, falleth alike upon the blest and upon the unblest, but the quality of mercy that falleth on the elected ain't in no way like that which falleth on the unelected. One will go to Washington, Charleston, Sacramento, Olympia, or someplace somewhat similar and probably double his foldin' money. The other will tuck his embarrassment under his wing and sneak back home to sponge off his friends--if he has any left.

No one else goes down to the ignominy of defeat quite like a politician who has been putting his mouth where his money is. And on television, of all places. He may try chewing on his sneakers which got stuck in some place where they shouldn't have been.

I've heard of one or two newspaper columnists and three or four television news commentators who had to do that enough times that they developed a taste for shoe leather. As for me, I would never attempt to predict the outcome of either an election or a rooster fight. And I absolutely would not wager my wages on the outcome.

It is pretty hard to ignore the primaries, but people in general have a tendency to forget them rather easily. Politicians have even shorter memories than people.

I don't want to mention any names after the goal posts have been torn down, but I heard one politician get right up there on TV in front of Ted and everybody and say that he now believed that the fellow who had tromped all over him in the primary was a fine man and should be elected. Less than five months earlier the same talker was saying that the talkee was as crooked as a hyena's hind leg and wasn't fit to hold office. That talker must have been lying at one time or another. Maybe the talkee had seen the light and changed his stripes. He hadn't changed the animal symbol which was still behind both their names.

I'll try to ignore the primaries in my own calculator-produced figures on costs for the elections. Some things, like recent primaries, are pretty hard to ignore, but I'll try. Some figures may have been reported short. My calculator (the one under that fuzzy spot just above my neck) only goes to ten places, so don't put too much stock in my figures. My seventy-two syndrome has interfered with my hearing.

Total expenditures in the nationally televised campaigns for one-state elections such as senatorial, congressional, and gubernatorial races accounted for something close to one billion dollars, give or take a few million here and there. The minor races were mere chicken feed. The only reason that they topped the former is that there were so bloomin' many more of the latter.

Let's take one of those sophisticated wild crabapple guesses (I know the terminology--I just don't use it) at about how much the minor leaguers spent and say another billion. Both of those figures are highly conservative, even if nearly half the candidates were liberal.

That makes 2 with a bunch of zeroes behind. I can't remember how many.

Based on recent (1993) population estimates, we have just over two hundred million people of voting age. That may include a few who swam in. About forty percent of those vote on a day when there is no rain and when political enthusiasm is running something above the barometic pressure and when they aren't too busy shooting pool or watching football or the 1994 World Series. Let's say a top of eighty million who are willing to make an X or punch holes in a computer card.

That means that politicians, successful and not quite, spent individually and collected at least twenty-five dollars per voter.

That sounds to me like a pretty high price to pay us for something we should have been doing anyway.

TRUE STORY DEPARTMENT:

We had a fellow in our town who was not quite fortunate enough to get as much as a first-grade education. No slur intended, but he was an unstaunch Republican. He wended his way to the polls back in the days when X's were in style and was met there by a neighbor who was of the same political faith.

That man went over the sample ballot carefully and explained that the X was to go under the eagle. It was definitely not to go under the rooster.

When the voter came out, the fellow met him to be sure his instructions were followed to the letter. In this case the letter was X. He asked the voter where he put his X. The response was,"I put it right there under that ------ chicken. That's the S.O.B. we want out of there."

The Turkey Drovers

I'll bet that not many of my readers have heard of a practice that was a little less than uncommon in these parts not quite a century ago.

I am proud to have as one of my readers a young lady who just celebrated her one-hundred-fourth birthday in February of this year. She is Mrs. Faye Garrison of High Point, N.C., a native of Auburn in Ritchie County. She taught for many years in that area. She may have taught some of my closer relatives at one time or another.

She was pictured on Willard Scott's portion of the Today Show on February 28, so I guess it is all right for me to tell her age.

I have never met her, but if God is willing and the creeks don't rise, I plan to sneak across the border and get down to the country of the Catawbas and Cherokees to see her before the summer is out.

She purchased a copy of my funny book, "The Berdine Un-Theory of Evolution and Other Scientific Studies Including Hunting, Fishing, and Sex" this past spring. After she read the book the first time and was able to bring her laughter under control, she started writing to me faithfully. We are still corresponding, even after she read it the second time to be sure that she had read right what I wrote.

She relayed to me a story from her teaching experience. It took place more than eighty years ago, so

187

it is history. One of those little dabs that was hidden behind the door of the print shop when the books were passed out. It was told once in The Parkersburg,W. Va. News-Sentinel, but it merits repeating.

She was a teacher in a one-room school with all eight grades huddling around the Burnside to keep warm.

One day during school hours when the kids were supposed to be learning how to tell the difference between an A and a Z and all of the letters between, she heard a commotion outside. What it was was a racket that sounded like the end was in sight. She ran to the window to see if she needed to do something to protect her proteges, some of which were likely bigger than she.

She immediately gathered the roomful of youngsters, all sixteen of them, and hustled them to the front porch to witness the spectacle.

A few guys were driving a flock of turkeys to market in much the same way the old-timey cowboys drove cattle except for three or four minor details.

One was the lack of horses. The drovers were riding Shank's Mare. Another was something that no cowboy in his right mind would ever think of doing and I doubt that many turkey drovers did it. The lead birds all sported long beards. They were fastened together with long boards which had been fashioned into yokes, four gobblers to the plank.

Those birds couldn't race to one side without all of them planning a frontal escape. If you know anything at all about turkeys, you know that they have to be the most stupid creatures that ever walked on two feet. You know that they could never do anything together. Those groups of lead turkeys walked along just as if they knew what they were doing. The rest of the flock trotted along behind the lead birds just as peacefully as you please.

I'll bet good money that most of those kids never forgot that sight.

We still send a few to market these days, but travel accommodations are improved. The birds today ride in style aboard an eighteen-wheeler. Practically every one I have seen climbing off the truck in recent years has been stripped bare and was frozen as stiff as a board.

I will admit that I have observed a load now and then zipping along faster than turkeys were ever meant to fly with their feathers flying hither, thither, and yon with no turkey attached. The feathers which were still on the crated birds weren't doing a whole lot to keep the turkeys warm. They were ruffled, to say the very least.

The climax to that story is that she was suspended for teaching the kids something worthwhile.

One of the problems with teaching is that everyone who never got past the sheep which was the keeper of the skin knows more about teaching than the teacher. And they are always vocal. The vocabulary is limited to words of criticism and never praise. They have probably forgotten that if it hadn't been for some teacher along the way, they wouldn't have had one. Vocabulary, that is.

The story had a happy ending. It happened before the days of school boards. The pseudo-board of education was a Board of Trustees composed of three people from the community. One of those was her father. She was reinstated by a vote of two to one without any loss of her twelve dollars a month salary. The kids lost three days of her valuable teaching.

Education has changed. I'm not sure it is better, but the kids today have much more to learn. We have the benefit of eighty more years of history and a few machines to take the place of brains. The machines can remember better.

If a teacher today had an opportunity to give her class an "eyeballs-on" educational experience like that, she would be reprimanded if she missed it.

But the union would see to it that she couldn't be fired.

Cable Television

I have been at it again--watching the news on television. This time it was on NBC News, being aired over the local NBC affiliate, WVVA-TV in Bluefield, another of my favorite professors in my continuing classes in adult education.

You could never guess what NBC's commentator told me was happening now.

The same people who were gung-ho for violating the constitutional rights of law-abiding gun owners are beginning to squeal like a stuck shoat.

It seems that some of Willie the Wisp's cohorts are trying to tell the television cable industry what stations they can (and conversely cannot) carry.

The very first squawk that erupted was, "That is unconstitutional." They cited the first amendment.

So, what else is new?

I can solid guarantee you that when the founding fathers wrote the first amendment, they weren't talking about television cable companies. I can also guarantee you that when they wrote the second, they were talking about the individual's right to keep and bear arms.

The anti-gun media and their far-left associates have tried to twist the wording of the second to mean that only an organized militia could do so.

That is pure hogwash. The only organized militia of that time and immediately preceding may have been called an army, but it was nothing more than a bunch of old hillbillies from the seashore and the adjacent flatlands and hillsides who had learned how to shoot while rabbit hunting (moving targets) and squirrel hunting (sitting targets) and how to hide behind rocks and trees while deer hunting.

If you get right down to the nitty gritty, that's what our "militia" is today. Some of the regular members may not know a squirrel from a rabbit, but they still use the same basic system to learn to shoot.

I started writing to newspapers and to television stations and networks several years ago. I was trying to convince those media which were constantly misrepresenting gun owners and harping for a dissembling of the Bill of Rights through gun control that as soon as someone planted a hard-toed boot in the rear of the second amendment, the first would collapse atop the rubble.

Bill Clinton, Jay Rockefeller, Sarah Brady, Bob Dole, Mario Cuomo, Ronald Reagan, Janet Reno, nor anyone else rules this country. The Constitution rules this country through the common people like you and me. Every time a church member, a farmer, a pet owner, a businessman, or a newspaperman shies away from his responsibility to preserve and to protect the rights of another citizen, he is endangering his own.

When a president, a legislator, a politician, or a judge infringes upon the rights of any individual, he also abrogates yours.

I recently wrote a bit of satire entitled "Putty Tats and Puppy Dogs." If you missed it, dig it out and read it. If the Congress, the President, and a bunch of nutty people can squeeze through useless legislation which, under the guise of crime control, takes away the right of a person who wants to own a gun, "it follows as night the day" that it won't be long before they can take away your right to own a home, a car, or a pet.

If they can punish law-abiding citizens by restricting gun ownership except to felons, they can certainly restrict or take away the supposed rights of a supposedly free press, the supposed rights of worship, the supposed rights of property owners, or anyone else they suppose to have rights under the Constitution.

They have already started nibbling. They are now beginning to bite the media where it smarts.

Henry Et a Crow
(I Didn't--I'm Chicken!)

Every now and again I have to give my eyeballs a respite from watching the flickering tube. Too much TV can cause you to develop dementia praecox, especially if you start believing everything you think you see and hear.

If you sit in a recliner or recline on a settee while you are watching, you will eventually notice another serious ailment--increaso girtho. Drinking some of the stuff from the sponsors of sporting events speeds up the process and results in another condition, maximus beltum shrinkus. It becomes harder and harder to make both ends meet.

Reading newspapers won't do that to you. You can get your morning constitutional by running out in a cold rain to look under the shrubbery for the morning news. You can't learn much from television that you hadn't already heard by word of rumor, but reading newspapers can give you the equivalent of an advanced degree from an accredited institution of higher learning. You may need to read between the lines.

I wouldn't want to mislead you, so I'm going to tell you a true story (I think) that began down in that little patch of woods that butted its butts up against our hillside corn patch. The kind of corn our cows ate and all my uncles sipped from a brown jug or a fruit jar in order to get their MDR of vitamins and minerals.

194

Well, most of it is true. My old and feeble mind plays tricks with my memory and this happened away back there B.C. (Before College), well over fifty years ago.

We were just beginning to emerge from the depths of everyone elses' Great Depression. We didn't have one of our own. We thought that life was supposed to be that way.

We hunted year 'round for wild meat and vegetables. I can't recall having time to just go for the fun of it. There was always a purpose to our hunting. Enhanced by an empty belly.

We rarely used a shotgun for anything but rabbits and only occasionally for those. The charge of little lead balls ruined too much eatin' meat and the store charge per load for 12 ga. shells was considerably more than for .22 LR's. We could miss eight or ten times with the hollow points and still be saving money.

All the groundhogs knew us by our Christian names in the summer and all the squirrels, rabbits, 'coons, and grouse soon learned them in the fall. Most years we started praying for a cold snap about the middle of August, not because of the heat, but because we were getting tired of wild greens and pot licker and wanted a change of diet.

We had a neighbor whose family was almost as well-off as ours. The man of the house had passed on some years before and they had to scrounge for food like all the rest of us only moreso. One of the older boys hunted year-round in his spare time.

Our spare time was plentiful. It came between walking from two to six miles each way to harass teachers, grubbing, planting, weeding, hoeing, thinning, cutting firewood, milking, preparing meals, washing dishes, and crawling on hands and knees between the rows of beans and potatoes to pick the bean beetles and potato bugs from their cozy hovels under the leaves of the plants. And heaven help us if we missed any nits. Those last two chores were to keep the dadblamed bugs from getting more to eat than we did.

We had free access to everybodys' land back in those days, so long as we closed the gates behind us and didn't ride down the fences. Henry had the same privileges.

He came up to our little patch of woods which cooked our meals and warmed our backsides to see if he could sneak up on a big old groundhog he had seen about a week earlier. Henry didn't know it, but that whistle-pig didn't dwell there any more. It had popped its head up to see what was happening in the outside world just as I laid the rifle barrel across a stump. His meat had gone to put a little more meat on our scrawny bones.

Henry waited behind the same clump of blackberry briers which had made such a good blind for me. He gave up after about three hours.

Just as he was ready to quit, an unwise crow lit in a tree at the edge of the woods, only a few yards away. Henry may have been desperate or terribly hungry. He let him have it. Crow might not be the same as groundhog but it might be better than chipmunk.

196

Henry must have been on the verge of starvation. He took the bird home with him and turned it into chicken and dumplings.

Then he told me about it. I asked him how it tasted. Henry said it didn't have a whole lot of flavor, even after he chewed a bite of the tender breast for more than ten minutes. He said that the gravy was too tough to chew.

He convinced me. I'm sticking with chicken. I might associate with a turkey or two now and then, but I ain't eatin' any crow. Not the feathered kind.

Sinning is what you caught someone else doing today that you didn't get caught doing yesterday.

The National Endowment for the Arts

I've been in front of the television set again. If I keep this up, you're going to think that I don't do much else.

I have been sidelined for the last few weeks because of some simple surgery which caused me to lighten my lift loads, if not my work load. I have been loafing around a little more than usual, letting my neighbors mow the lawn, allowing my wife to take out the garbage, asking the grocery clerks to load my purchases, and having someone else carry everything except my money. I'd probably let them do that if it weren't for the fact that it doesn't exceed the weight limit for my lifting.

I was watching an attractive lady on C-Span early this morning. She was celebrating her third day on the job as chairman of The National Endowment for the Arts. I can't seem to become accustomed to saying chairwoman or chairperson, but one look at her and anybody with any depth perception at all would know that she isn't a man. I could tell that right off.

I didn't hear her raise any objection to any title. She may have known all along that such designations would not have any effect on the eye of the beholder. The interviewer may have called her "Director." Whatever anyone calls her will be immaterial. She will have her work cut out for her. She will be besieged by persons claiming to be artists and by other persons who are delighted that they aren't.

She will be swamped with material that doesn't come close to being art and by material which is really pornography or obscenity wearing one of Art's old hats. I'll gamble that a whole world of things which are really works of art but not viewed as such will go unheeded.

Take coal mining for instance. Coal mining is definitely a work of art, especially if it is to pay its own way. Ditch digging with a mattock and shovel is almost a lost art. Any person who can dig a straight ditch with the proper slope is a real artist. Try it sometime. Stacking hay is another lost art. Oh, there may be one or two old farmers around who still do it for the sake of precious memories, but it is lost to most of us. Machine-baled hay may do the job better, but a bunch of round bales of hay shoved off into one corner of the field just doesn't have the same esthetic value as a stackpole with hand-piled hay around it.

Most men take it for granted, but housekeeping is a work of art if it is done properly. I speak with authority on that subject. I tried it once more than fifty years ago. I can solid guarantee you that I am no artist. My housekeeping furnished me with a great incentive to search 'til I could find someone better qualified.

The primary difference between me and some of those people who pass off their work as art is that I am willing to admit that mine isn't.

I do a lot of criticizing of various government programs which spend my hard-earned Social Security checks and your lottery winnings for projects and boondoggles which have absolutely no merit. I probably include one once in a while that does have a little merit, especially if that merit is hidden behind a bunch of gobbledy-gook and bureaucratic doublespeak.

I have ripped into, on a nationwide basis, the funding for the study of the sex life of tree frogs, the overfunding of peanut farmers, the study of the environmental impact of bovine intestinal gases (I wonder why they didn't include horses.), the National Biological Survey (pending), and at least two or three other equally worthwhile projects. One of those targets has been the NEA. Not the entire gamut of art funded by the NEA, just some aspects.

Some of the so-called art that has come out of such funding is blatantly anti-God and anti-Christ. If that same "artist" had painted a minority subject in the same sort of depiction, he would have been spending all the rest of his life painting scenes with bars in front of them. Depicting bodily excretory functions is not art, regardless of the eyes of the beholder. It is nothing more than filth being purveyed as art.

Nearly everyone knows about such necessary bodily functions. I'll bet there isn't one person in a thousand who considers his last trip to the john as a work of art. Relief maybe, but not art.

I believe that art has a definite place in our lives. I believe that some of the works sponsored or funded by the NEA are worthwhile, especially when it funds legitimate activities for communities which could not afford them otherwise.

I also believe that we are seeing a slow but steady evolutionary process in which the bureaucrats and politicians are manipulating our media. The increase in our national immorality can be directly linked to the use of the media by the liberal left. We have seen a steady decline in the quality of programming on television since the sixties. If you have been watching the news programs recently, you probably have had the feeling they are sort of lopsided, canted strongly to the left.

Several of our better-known newspapers continue to emphasize the liberal views over the conservative. Legislation is now in place to require conservative papers and TV programs to give at least equal time to liberal coverage. That jogging shoe could be on the other foot before they get the velcro fastened.

What some people call art is not exactly what most of us backwoods Mountain Williams consider as being on a level with a Raphael, a Rembrandt, or a Renoir. In case you are wondering what a Mountain William is, that's just a sophisticated hillbilly. If you are now wondering what a sophisticated hillbilly is, that is one who would rather have a genuine imitation of one of the above hanging over his mantel or Buck Stove than a genuine Mexican Velvet.

If you have seen a picture of just about any side street in New York City that was taken in the last couple of decades, you could not help but wonder about the "art" which is smeared all over the private and public buildings. We have some of that genre here in West Virginia. Ours is smeared on otherwise beautiful rocks, crags, bridges, overpasses, outhouses, and where have you.

I cannot see the beauty in a sign spray-painted by some person who obviously never learned to write which says, "LB luvs RM," or by one who must have sort of which says, "Jimmy loved Tammy and Sadie and Mary and Johnny and Charley."

I don't like to see religious messages there either. There is something about a sign painted on a roadside rock face which says, "Jesus Wept" that turns me every way but on. I have a sneaking suspicion that He might have when He saw someone smearing cheap paint on a part of God's creation. I can't believe that He would want that kind of advertising, even if the motive was of the highest caliber.

I want to wish Jane Alexander the best of everything in her new job, especially the art.

She will need all our prayers.

Male Smoking and Male Impotence Connected (or What Some of Us Have Suspected for Years)

Recent newspaper headlines and television newscasts have been announcing an amazing discovery. Those little rascals which we called Coffin Nails when I was a boy and when we weren't calling them something worse are now being blamed for one more human deficiency. It may be more of a threat to sales than lung cancer and heart disease combined.

It may result in farmers finding an alternate money-maker. They may, under the recently passed Global Agreement on Trade and Tariff (GATT for those of you who want to shorten it), start shipping bales of 'baccy to China, Japan, India, other parts of Asia, Europe, and Africa where they really need it. On the other hand, there may be millions of men who will buy a couple of cartons for each of their friends, thereby boosting sales to an all-time high. I strongly suspect there will be a significant increase in numbers of men who pull one out, light up, and then lay it down to smolder and to choke the guy in the next booth, directly in the slip stream. Some people will stoop to anything to get ahead of the competition.

The discovery may be the third strike for the third out in the bottom of the ninth for the home team (the tobacco industry) which is already trailing by two runs and losing fans tips over trash. Tobacco growers will know what those are.

203

People who smoke cigarettes seem not to worry too much about the consequences of lung cancer, heart disease, or a myriad of other problems which can arise from puffing on the wrong end. Those are long-range problems and won't appear until five or six years in the future. This new (?) deficiency may happen much sooner than a man is ready for it.

I haven't had time to do much research on the problem among females of the species. I'm just like all the other pollsters and get my bona fide answers by asking questions. I have taken my own polls on such things as Gun Control (four people), NAFTA (two), The National Endowment for the Arts (three), and The Undercover Life of the American Female (I never got past the first house).

I may just pass up this splendid opportunity to poll them this time for scientific research, since I already know what the answers will be. Dr. Kinsey and Jim Comstock did that some years back. Kinsey did it nationwide, Jim limited his research to Richwood.

I'm not sure what questions they asked, but I do know what they said some of the answers were. I doubt if they asked the woman of the house if she hid her husband's smokes on a regular basis. The females may not be ready for it to happen either.

This "new" discovery indicates that something in the tobacco smoke from cigarettes adversely affects a man's libido, get-up-and-go, potency, or whatever else you choose to call it.

I have not conducted any comprehensive scientific tests to determine just how or why the primary pollutant in cigarette smoke does such a dastardly thing to a man. I did not hear mentioned by those who had how it might affect the urge in females. There may be room for a discrimination case. If you can whip up a smart lawyer. Be sure to listen to see if he has a cigarette cough.

I am absolutely certain of one thing. I quit smoking homemade cigarettes just after I reached my twelfth birthday and not too long after I had graduated from field blossom and corn silk. I learned the hard way that they can cause another affliction which has seldom been mentioned in the media. They will wear out the seat of a pair of bib overalls more than twice as fast as normal and put red welts on the portion of skin which hides just beneath the patches. The pain goes right to the seat of learning.

I, for one, am glad the researchers have been working like busy little bees and discovered this fault of nicotine in the nick of time.

I just knew there had to be one more good reason for not smoking.

Surgeon General Had Foot-in-mouth Disease

I was sitting in the foyer of the gift shop at the Tourist Information Center near Princeton Friday evening during the Christmas on the Parkways open house, autographing books and almost minding my own business.

Two of my loyal fans and readers, former Governor Hulett Smith and his wife Nancy, came in and made a bee-line for my desk. They are two of the finest of fine West Virginians.

They have enjoyed my political satire for several years, especially those columns in which I got on the Surgeon General like ugly on an ape because of her off-hand and off-color remarks. I think that she must sleep with a foot in her mouth and inserts the other one between her dentures on a regular basis.

Hulett had heard the news on television and could hardly wait to spring it on me. I had been deprived of the comforting glare of the habit-forming tube for nearly six hours and was suffering withdrawal symptoms. I could not have heard about the unlove of my life. She had done it again--jammed her mouth into high gear while her brain was idling in neutral.

Added to all the problems he had been having inside his own party and outside with the other one, it was more than Willie the Wisp could take. He put the heat on her to resign. She did. I rejoiced. I am tempted to start calling him President Clinton again.

He has been having more bad days lately than his Mama done tol' him to expect. Rumors started flying thick and fast that Lloyd Bentsen was about to retire. Lloyd is the Secretary that looks after all your money. He stood in front of the cameras and said that rumors of his retirement were pre-mature, something like the rumors circulated years ago about Mark Twain's death. There were firm denials right up to the minute the unfirm truth finally leaked out.

Ron Brown is leaving--if you can believe unfounded rumors which have an uncanny way of coming to pass.

Some of the Democratic Party wheels have started running scared. They are now butting heads with the President. If I know anything about hard heads, they might as well rejoin the party. They are blaming him for the recent unslide. Maybe they should look inward.

Boris put in his two rubles worth when he publicly reprimanded the very same fellow from whose pockets he had recently picked five megabucks of your tax money. Do you suppose he asked, "But what have you done for me lately?"

The recent election sent a passel of the President's left-hand men home to ponder their future and to worry about where their next lobster and T-bone dinner was coming from.

And on top of all that, his hand-picked female physician had to go and make a statement like that right up there on television where Fred, Ted, and everybody could read her lips. It's no wonder the poor guy got upset.

He did manage to squeeze in part of one good day with the help of Bob and Newt, of all people. The GATT which the 103rd Congress tabled just before the election in order to fool the voters and give the miners the shaft was passed with a show of hands. I watched as pens flew in all directions as he hurried to sign it before Congress had a chance to change its collective mind. He had the help of several Republicans who will take the Helms of the 104th.

I know that it says that you aren't supposed to look a gift horse in the mouth to see if it has dental caries, but maybe he should at least have asked that one to say, "Aaaaahhhhh." The Republicans were pretty foxy. If GATT turns out to be a good piece of parchment, they can hog most of the credit. If it lands bottom side up, they can blame the ex-liberals in the 103rd who furnished the writing paper for the President to practice his autograph.

The President's political popularity is right now lower than a hop toad's hindquarters. People with whom I have talked since the President took away Joycelin's scalpel and stethoscope and her free handouts to first graders have expressed their approval. Some went so far as to be enthusiastic.

His approval rating could soar faster than a monkey which backed into a hot Burnside if the media ever find out about the groundswell.

A 'Coon Huntin' Story

Since I retired and can eat breakfast 'most any time I take a notion, I have been going to Arby's once or twice a week during those weeks when I can hang my hat on the back of my own chair. I run into a few regulars who drop by there to take advantage of the old hillbilly discount and to chew their bacon over a cup or two of dark coffee. Hardly any really old hillbillies I know want their coffee any way but black.

One of the fellows told a story about a 'coon hunt which reminded me of a couple of things from my dim past which could have led up to it, so I know it must be true. I used to like to hear the dogs run 'coons. I also liked to hear them chase a red fox. I liked most the fun of sitting around and talking with the others who were just as enthusiastic as I was.

I once roamed the back roads in these mountains while calling on the mines in the area. Somebody told me that I was a salesman. I don't know whether he ever found out or not.

I was on a dirt road between Jenkinjones and Pocahontas one evening and heading for the barn with my tail up when I popped through a narrow spot between a big rock and a hard place and came upon a pickup with its bed full of cages.

I was there just as they were lifting the first cage to the ground. Being the curious (a soft word for nosy), person that I am, I stopped to watch and chat.

They had bought the 'coons in the Great Dismal Swamp area where 'coons were thicker than grasshoppers and brought them here where they could run and play without getting their feet wet. I watched them release about two dozen before I had to leave. It was a sight to behold to see the little rascals bolt from the cages and head for the creek.

The men were 'coon hunters and were stocking the area to provide sport in the fall. They were dedicated 'coon hunters. Like dedicated fox hunters, they don't hunt to kill. They get their jollies by listening to the dogs trying to unravel the twists and turns the 'coon made while trying to elude the dogs. I was reminded of a hilltop long ago and far away, so I understood.

The story the fellow told took place somewhat later. I like to think that they could have been listening to the dogs chase one of the little 'coons which I watched skedaddle into the brush. I have changed the names and the story a little to protect the guilty.

Hank, Jake, and Paul had hauled the dogs to the back side of the mountain. That mountain used to be full of bears, deer, turkeys, grouse, and rattlesnakes. It is still polluted with the rattlers, but the other animals are somewhat scarcer. They had seated themselves on a fallen tree just shy of midnight and were listening to the dogs making their mountain music. They had hunted the area so many times before that they could just about call any 'coon by name by the way he ran and the creeks he crossed to get to his hollow tree.

The snuff juice was flying and the mouthwash was flowing. Hank was arguing that his Old Jack was in the lead and working the 'coon back toward the hunters. The others were sure that it was their dogs in the lead.

Hank stopped in the middle of a sentence, grabbed his leg and circled it with his fingers just above his knee and let out a squall. "They's a d....rattlesnake done crawled up my overhaul leg. Git somethin' quick and git him outa there afore he bites me."

Jake grabbed a dead branch that was thicker than his arm and drew back. Paul yelled, "Whoa! Whoa! Don't hit him with that thing or you'll break his leg." Hank was holding on and looking at the stars as he prayed at the top of his voice. "Oh, Lord, don't let that d....snake bite me. I promise I'll quit my swearin'. I'll give up my Copenhagen. If you don't let him bite me, I'll even start going to church once in a while."

Paul told Jake to grab aholt of Hank's arm on that side and when he counted to three to start lifting Hank ever so easy. He told Hank not to move that leg whatever he did. Hank stopped praying long enough to yell, "I ain't a lettin' loose of that leg. I don't want that d....snake gettin' any higher."

They eased him into a one-legged standing position. All their camp lamps were focused on the overall leg that looked like it was alive. "He's a slippin, fellers. I can feel him a slippin' down." Hank spotted it first. "Lookee there, fellers. The Lord done changed that d....snake inter a frog."

Bill Clinton Decides (?) to Run

I have to be completely honest with you before you get the wrong impression from my writings. I really believe that Bill Clinton is a fairly decent man. Except for one or two minor faults which are entirely human. (See saw seen on page 197 and at top of next article).

I agree with one of his former high school classmates from the Razorback State who stopped to talk with me as she was on her way back home from a class reunion at The White House. She said that she liked him as a person.

It's his cotton-pickin' politics that I can't handle. She volunteered the information that she disagreed with his politics, too. I never met a Democrat nor a Republican I didn't like or could at least learn to abide. Why in tarnation did Bill Clinton have to be a Hillarycrat? That's why I started calling him Willie the Wisp even before he became President Clinton.

If you think I am kidding about Hillary's lopsided politics, you need to read up on her background. I can solid guarantee you that she did not inherit her political bent from her Pappy.

Willie hasn't lied nearly as much as some writers and commentators would have you believe. They were only telling what they heard and didn't probe beneath the surface. They didn't realize that he wasn't really lying. It was simply that Hillary kept changing her mind so quickly that he couldn't keep up with what she wanted

212

him to say. Some women are like that.

He would just seem to get his size 13's firmly planted at last in wet red clay when Hillary would tell him to do an about-face, mud, goo, and all. He wasn't too overly experienced in close-order drill.

There is a sizeable number of people who call ourselves columnists. Some of us keep our blurry eyes on Washington politics. Some of those eyes are only temporarily blurred, usually in morning-after hours. Others are like mine.

Some of the watchers observe carefully and report what they see on the surface. I may be the only one like me. I read what those others report and then dig a bit beyond the surface and make my reports, which may or may not be in line with the consensus among others. If it weren't for the careful watchers who tell me what to analyze, I would have to hang up my pencils and depend on subsidies for old and decrepit writers.

We were wondering, would Willie the Wisp run. We won't wonder longer. He pitched his left jogging shoe into the ring. (He doesn't wear a hat like all the other politicians, just a floppy baseball cap). He said so. Hillary said so.

I suppose most of us really knew he would. The first commentator who told me about it on television didn't raise more than one of her bushy eyebrows when she gave me the Hot News Flash. Later commentators weren't nearly so enthusiastic. They must have been scooped.

The President has been laying the groundwork ever since November 17 for another plunge into the political puddle. It took him that long to recover from the aftershocks of the election. He had been busy paying more attention to Hillary and hadn't realized that so many Americans didn't understand that higher taxes, higher spending, minority rule, losses of civil freedoms, and Hillaryism was good for them.

Newt and his cronies (those include some hard-line, old-time Democrats who don't want their names mentioned. Only one of them openly flopped.) came up with a proposal to reduce taxes on Americans who are caught in the middle, some of whom are not so middlin'.

The President jumped on that one with both clodhoppers. He gained a lap or two on old Newt who had run head-on into a wayward orphanage and was still picking splinters from his teeth. Newt will learn that you don't run into hot issues like that with your mouth open.

If Willie keeps on stealing Newt's thunder, he just might run disguised as a Republican.

Newt's Shoes Don't Fit Where He Puts Them

Someone once defined sin as the same thing that you catch somebody doing today that you were not caught while doing it yesterday. If you want to pin me down and force me to reveal who said it, I'll plead the fifth. And I never touch that stuff which comes packed solidly in that size.

Newt was caught sinning soon after the election. He put first one foot and then the other into that big cavity under where his mustache would be if he had one. He is still spitting leather and shoe polish from the orphanage fiasco, which may or may not have been precisely quoted. He had an expensive oxford on the other. He had considerable help from the electronic media on the first. He had help from some publisher on the second.

He had been offered a four million dollar advance on a book which wasn't written. It may not have been in the idea stage. That is more than they offered me NOT to publish mine. When Newt spit that one out, he had slow-talked his way out of the cash. He had help in both parties and the White House in extracting it. He needed all the help he could get. That wad of dollar bills would be bound to make a tight wedge.

I occasionally have feelings, call them hunches, sneaky suspicions, premonitions, ESP, or intestinal spasms (I don't use that other term in front of the kids.), which come upon me at the oddest times. I have at least three now that some of those critics had a bad dose of jitters. Newt was about to get rich quick. And after taxes at that.

The opposition couldn't have that happening again so soon. Ollie came too close to turning his book into a table-turner. If Newt could lay his hands on his own financing, it's hard to tell how he might turn out.

You have probably noticed that Newt's hair is turning prematurely gray. I suppose that is from excessive worrying. I have heard that will do it. If he continues opening his mouth to show his pearlies where the media is present, he may have more worries. It could cause him to have hair like mine. Most of it is still dark, I suppose. It surely wouldn't turn gray after it has fallen out.

One would think that a college professor who taught History, of all things, would know what happens when you talk too much. Even I know that, although I am still trying hard to break the habit. TV reporters sit around with a handful or two of words to toss into your mouth every time they see it fly open. Newspaper people would never do a thing like that.

The last time I saw him on television, he was still going strong. He was saying that he had turned down the four megabucks for the good of the party and the country. That is an admirable attitude.

One of the disloyal opposition made a few offhand remarks, saying that the publisher was a potential beneficiary of some possible future communications legislation.

He was blowing more blue smoke than an over-weight eighteen-wheeler dropping down Sandstone Mountain with the Jake-Brake engaged. He forgot to tell you about the recent administration-backed legislation which rewarded one newspaper with a 220 megabucks* boon and another communicator with just shy of a whole geigabuck*.

Newt's was mere chicken feed compared to those. And about half of his would have trickled into the Treasury pot through taxes. The biggie bites of biscuits and pork broth were sopped out of it.

It must be difficult for politicians to tell it like it is. It proves that just because you scratch their backs is no guarantee of getting your itch scratched back.

You can't tell me that politics and sin are stranger bedfellows.

*megabuck-1 million frogskins
*geigabuck-1,000 million ditto--roughly equal to one billion of them.

P.S. This was written before Newt's Mama met Connie Chung and whispered her secret into Connie's ear. Ten minutes later, she learned that Connie can't keep a secret. She will likely be more careful about what she tells whom that Newty said.

She can trust me.

217

Rewriting History

I was leaning back in my recliner last evening with my feet propped up as high as they would go and watching the news flashes on the screen which was framed between my socks.

It is amazing how much you can learn from that position if you can manage to tear yourself away from the other programs which feature a steady diet of sex, violence, and vulgarity. My TV has an automatic filtering device to keep such stuff out of my house. It is called a forefinger. I keep one of my two poised over the remote at all times.

I just heard a brief news item about a new un-history text which is being considered for schools nationwide by some bureaucrats in Washington who have gained some notoriety for their undercover work and for their propensity for half truths and outright lies. That is only hearsay.

I heard it only once. That alone is like waving a red flag at a color-blind under-suspicious old bull like me.

That new textbook (?) was reported as omitting such historical figures from our past as George Washington and Robert E. Lee, among others. If it hadn't been for Colonel (later General and President) George, General "Lighthorse" Harry Lee, and several others, we would not have had an American History to study. We would more than likely still be speaking English with a British accent and priming our minds to pay homage to Prince

Charles if General George had stayed in Mount Vernon with his toes toasting in front of the grate instead of getting them frostbitten at Valley Forge.

My Great-great-great-grandpa Berdine isn't so much as mentioned in the new book. Come to think of it, I don't believe that he was mentioned in the old ones, either, but he was there.

General George and Grandpa B. were both in that 400-year-long war which some historians call "The Indian Wars." It started before 1500 and lasted until Wounded Knee. You won't get a heated argument from me if you insist that it is still going, although not quite so bloody as it once was. They took part in the segments known as The French and Indian War, Lord Dunmore's War, and the American Revolution. Only three of my ancestors made it into the important history books of the time.

General Robert E. Lee, a former Union man, made a place in American History by turning the Big War into a rout at Gettysburg. His. He made his second big mistake when he surrendered his sword to Grant at Appomattox. We have been paying for that one ever since. So has he. He alone was denied reinstatement of citizenship. I have never understood why.

Grandpa wasn't there for that one. When it started with a few practice shots from an antique artillery piece, he was still trying to fast-talk St. Peter into opening the gate a crack and going to the tobacco shop for a good cigar so he could maybe sneak in.

The un-history, according to reports I have heard and read, attempts to distort Thanksgiving by saying that the Pilgrims were giving thanks to the Indians instead of to God. Hogwash! The Indians deserved the gratitude of the settlers, but that is a bit different.

An earlier rewrite of non-history tried to teach your kids that the Pilgrims came to this country because they liked to wander, not because of religious persecution.

I sat with both hands under my skinny seat so that I wouldn't jump out of my balcony seat and punch some puny Harvard professor on his drippy nose. He was giving a commencement address and lying through his dentures about The War Between the States. He was telling the college graduating class that slavery was the cause of that fiasco. They didn't know any better.

He went so far as to say that his state was on the side of Right. He didn't know what the squabble was about. He neglected to tell the group that every state was a slave-holding state at one time or another before the hassle started. He neglected to tell the crowd that slavery had been on the way out, even in the tallest cotton, for nigh on to sixty years before the first assault rifle lobbed that big lead pumpkin at Fort Sumter.

Slavery was wrong. I doubt that I'll get any argument on that. It was wrong 5000 years ago and it is still just as wrong today and all the time between. So was that war. But changing history is just as wrong. Such distortions and omissions do absolutely nothing to promote racial harmony. They do aggravate dissension.

You don't have to be a whole lot older than me to recall how Russia's pre-Marxist history changed after Lenin's boys and girls raised a ruckus.

They tried to make the unpleasant years of Tsarist rule disappear by pretending they never happened. You know how well it worked.

It is happening right here and now. In the good old U.S. of A. The un-history group is attempting to destroy a belief in American heroes, some of whom gave their lives to preserve the freedom to believe in the nation and in its heroes. Some of them did have feet of clay. But name me one in any other country who didn't.

I realize that kids have much more history to learn today, but if they don't learn the accurate history of our past, they will have no basis in the future upon which to avoid the mistakes of that past.

I poke a little fun at history on occasion. I tell up front that is what I am doing. It is called fiction. I do not approve of passing fiction off on to school kids as fact. They are going to have a hard enough time trying to straighten out the messes we have left for them without our snowing them under with half-truths.

And You Thought I Was Only Kidding

I recently saw and heard two things on that major of all mediums where I get all my adult education in political science and a couple of other subjects. They should make every American, no matter if he bleeds red, blue, or slightly pink, sit up and take notice.

The first news flash was about the amazing increase in numbers and political influence of that group which most of the media calls "The Religious Right." It is always called that mistakenly and, almost as often, with a sort of sneer on its lip, at the tip of its pencil, or in its voice, as if the people who believe in America are somehow playing too far off base.

That group has become active in the political arena. And not a minute too soon. It sat on its collective hands while the tenets upon which this country was founded were being stolen from under its very noses. It has now accomplished some astonishing upsets in some of the oddest places.

It may be that the best thing which will come out of the present and previous administrations will be that cementing together of the various groups which have been trying to preserve your rights while they were going it alone. That cohesion among those groups is essential if our rights are to be maintained.

"The Religious Right" is not first a religious group. It is primarily a collection of those groups dedicated to preserving the rights of individuals guaranteed by the

222

Constitution. Those rights have been gradually eroded and usurped by the very people we have elected to represent us. It is true that many of its members are also members of an organized church or other religious group, but that seems to be coincidental. It is also true that the moving force behind that cohesion may have been "The Christian Coalition."

"The Religious Right" has caused members of both houses of Congress to start shaking in their collective oxfords. The reverberations are going to be felt in both major parties. The people are sending a clear message which our elected representatives don't want to hear. That message from the majority is so simple that it goes over the heads of those who are avidly seeking a "one-world" government or self-aggrandizement. It is only, "Start representing us and stop telling us what we should and should not think."

Some of those left-of-center politicians are already crying foul. I heard at least one of them proclaim, "But I am a Christian, too." I know absolutely nothing about him beyond that declaration. He may have been telling the truth, but he is missing the point entirely.

The interpretation of the purpose and the message is wrong. The purpose of the group is to preserve individual and group rights. The message is, "Start doing it now."

It is not about religion, or whether a person is a Christian, a Jew, a Muslim, or something else. It is about the RIGHT to be.

It *is* about the application of Lincoln's words, "...that government *of* the people, *by* the people, *for* the people," with a strong accent on the prepositions.

No wonder the incumbents are becoming nervous. With their records of rights violations, they should be quaking in their skivvies.

The second tid-bit ties in with the first. Pro-lifers have been check-reined by the Supreme Court's decision saying that legitimate protestors against the infant murder and feticide must stand back at least thirty-six feet from the scenes of the crimes. I would like for some prudent judge to explain to this unlearned hillbilly how thirty-six feet is a proper distance and why any yardstick should be used to fit the Freedom of Speech and Peaceful Assembly. That decision can only lead to illegal actions by those who are zealots, but looking for an excuse to take any course to halt or deter what they see as injustices. It can only lead to more bloodshed.

I'll bet my bottom dollar that they will never find pro-abortionists and rowdy rioters guilty of violating that standard. They want to give the latter medals for standing inside and swiping.

The First Amendment is no more specific than the second. I can solid guarantee you that the Founding Fathers did not have television in mind when they wrote it. I can also guarantee you that they did have arming the citizenry in mind when they wrote the Second, and especially the last phrase.

It was not to protect the country from outside forces. We had just gone through a period of protesting our own government and the ensuing rebellion against that government. It was placed there to insure that there would be some recourse against future tyranny.

The Right stood by with their hands in their pockets while the Second was being hacked to pieces by the experts at smoke-bombing. The media furnished the rooting section.

I wonder what will happen now that the First is showing more signs of toppling atop the rubble of the Second.

P.S. This column was written long before the 1994 elections. That show of hands resulted in the first turnaround in Congress in forty years. It was hailed as an unforeseeable upset. Malarkey!

The politicos are still trying to determine the real cause. They had better study their history. Foreign and Domestic.

Everyone Should Make New Year's Resolutions

If you have any desire at all to improve your mind or that big chunk of human flesh which holds it off the ground and out of the gutter, you need to think about how to do it. One good first step is to make New Year's Resolutions. If you are already perfect like some of the rest of us, they are just a waste of time.

The New Year seems to be a good time to turn over a new leaf on something besides the calendar. There is a definite cut-off date when we do away with the old. Except for the Christmas bills which we acquired when we spent a mite too much. There is a definite cut-on date for beginning the new. The change-over is accentuated by pulling the old calendar off the nail and hanging another in its place, if you are lucky enough to find a company which is prosperous enough to be able to hand out free ones. If you have to buy one, examine it carefully, and don't grab one which appears to have had a year's worth of eyeballing. Those aren't worth toting home. Most of the numbers look the same, but if you pay careful attention, they have changed.

The numbers will change even more in another six years, if you can hang around that long to see it.

Most people make resolutions. They manage to keep them for about six hours or until they sober up, whichever comes first. I believe that all depends upon your willpower and upon your wisdom in choosing resolutions which are not too hard to keep.

I try to make resolutions which can't be easily broken. I promise every year, for example, to quit smoking cigarettes. That is an admirable goal. My mother helped me with that one exactly sixty years ago last July. It was on a Sunday and no where near to New Year's Day on either side. I remember it as though it were yesterday. I still reach behind me to feel the area to see if there are still any welts. I haven't mauled a Marlboro, coughed over a Chesterfield, choked on a Camel, or lighted up a Lucky since.

I am making several new resolutions this year. Some of them are beginning to look a little dog-eared and ragged around the edges. I want to share them with you. I thought that if I told you, it might give me a greater incentive to keep them. And they just might inspire you to make a few and keep them.

I resolve for this new year:

To eat more ramps than last year.

To go fishing more often, or if I can't find time to go, to at least think about it.

To save my money for the more important and essential things of life--like plugs, spinners, flies, nightcrawlers, live minnows, etc. I might even buy a new rod and reel. The new ones I got my wife for Christmas last year are beginning to show signs of wear. The ones I got her for our anniversary look as though they might be suffering from overuse.

To never do today what I put off until tomorrow yesterday.

To mow the lawn more regularly--unless I am too busy talking, fishing, running up and down the dirt mountain roads, fishing, tuning up the boat motor, fishing, or taking catnaps in the recliner.

To never step off the bank on to a full-grown tree which is on its side in the water. I did that last year. That's how I got my new J. B. Stetson wet. One second I was standing on dry ground, eyeballing the eighty-foot long smooth trunk and the roots to be sure they were firmly anchored. The next I was trying to reach wet bottom so I could shove my Stetson back into the frosty air where it belonged. It was about two feet under the surface of the small lake in Canada with all of me hanging underneath its brim.

P.S. I survived. I also learned that it sure is easy to pray fervently with your mouth shut.

To laugh more and to try to get others to laugh. With me or at me, it makes no difference. Life is too short and the living of it too serious to be taken seriouly.

To keep an open mind about the administration regardless of who is sitting in the swivel seat. As soon as my mind is open, I plan to jump all over them with both pencils, whether it be the Lower House, the Upper House, or the White House. I hope you all will let me keep you posted on some of their goings-on.

And to wish you all a Happy, Healthy, Peaceful, and Prosperous New Year!

Hillside Serenades and Flatland Shivarees

I hope you will join this old man in a little reminiscing and rambling about a practice which has all but disappeared from our lives.

You old-timers will likely remember the rousing serenades we had when we were a few years younger. You new-timers ought to stick around long enough to learn about them. So you will know enough not to revive the custom.

I was born and reared in the hill country where the hillsides were so steep you had to build a stone wall to keep the onions from rolling out of bed. Everywhere we went was either up or down. The tipped terrain caused us to find entertainment near by rather than walk the six or eight miles to town. It cost more to shoot pool or see a movie there than we could afford. I don't want you to think we were poor, but even the moonshiners and bootleggers in our pitiful parcels didn't have any money. They kept pretty busy swapping.

We kept a weather-eye peeled for couples who looked as though they were about to be married. Sometimes you could tell. We kept our ears to the wind and tuned to the gossip, just in case our eyes weren't sharp enough. A marriage was an excuse for some top entertainment, a serenade or a shivaree. The name depended upon which side of the big holler the bride lived.

We had a few people who could fiddle around with a violin, pluck a guitar, plunk a banjer, or blow into a harmonica. Once in a while, only the fiddler showed.

The first thing we did at a serenade was to start a square dance. Some of us even danced round. Most of us waited for the women before we started.

Our square dances weren't the kind they do today. Those are imported from Texas, California, and places like that. Ours were converted to hill country from the jigs of Ireland, the schottisches of Scotland, and maybe a hornpipe or two. The calls were strictly country.

We had an old fellow who had been happily married for more years than most of us had been alive. His wife had gone ahead to fry his taters and side meat and to boil his morning coffee. She would have the table set and breakfast waiting when he made his way through the pearly gates.

He wasn't much of a hand at cooking and house-keeping. He had done the plowing, the planting, and the reaping while she saw to the milking and the housework. When she left him behind, he soon discovered that he needed help. Lots of help.

It just so happened that a woman in the area had lost her husband. She was just like Old Al, only exactly opposite. She needed a man. I'm not sure for what. She also needed a permanent place to place her head at night. Al offered her the job of housekeeper. She accepted. She lived in. They finally decided to marry to keep down the gossip, if for no other reason.

I don't think it was a shotgun wedding, but several fellows showed up carrying theirs. With white bows.

The wedding took place in the parlor. The serenade was held just after the preacher made his exit, which as I recall, was made rather hastily. He couldn't handle such large crowds.

He wasn't out of sight before the jugs appeared as if by miracle. The fiddle, guitar, banjo, and harmonica appeared almost simultaneously.

There were enough females to furnish partners for the boys to fill all rooms with sets, so into it we went. Al and Molly danced as though there might not be another tomorrow. The dancing lasted for about five hours. I'm not sure if it outlasted the moonshine. A few of the guys were hitting the floor pretty hard with their feet.

The dancing stopped when a couple of guys showed up with a mop, a bucket of something that looked a lot like tar, and an old feather pillow. Everyone thought they were plumb serious and plumb pickled. They managed to get Al and Molly outside. One look could reveal that they weren't relishing the idea. When one of the men sopped the mop in the tar, he broke up and sobered up immediately. Al and Molly weren't the only ones who heaved a sigh.

The men did get a rail to take Al for a short ride around the barn lot. Not as many fence rails were rotten back then. Before they could catch Al, Molly jumped up on the rail and told them to ride her. Al was forgotten. She rode it all the way. Then Al took his turn. I suppose they thought that would end the horse-play and the serenade.

The crowd hung around until long after midnight. Al and Molly were anxious to get to bed. They must have been sleepy.

Molly finally gave the kids the last of the candy. That was the signal for us to leave. It was time for Al and Molly to get on with their new life.

My wife and I have spent considerable time in that northern country where everybody speaks two languages, one of which isn't Spanish and the other isn't either. We are usually chasing a funny-looking fish which bites our lures so we can bite him back.

We were in Quebec for an extended period doing some research. We met a woman who had been reared in New York. She moved to Quebec when she was twelve. She had forgotten how to speak English. She did not know a single word.

My daughter and I took on the job of trying to teach her at least some. We succeeded in teaching her several sentences. The second summer of our tutoring was when the story took place. By that time we were full-fledged friends and confidantes of the family.

She married a Frenchman from Quebec. She knew how to say "Oui." They raised a family of seventeen youngsters. Then they learned that some clerk had goofed. They weren't legally married.

Some people I know would leap at such a chance. Not those two. They decided to do it again, priest and all. I doubt they planned another family that size. We

232

were invited to the wedding and to the shivaree which was to follow. Complete with square dance. That place was country, twenty-eight miles to the nearest town.

The trio played all the old French favorites like Turkey in the Straw, Arkansas Traveler, Red Wing, and Old Joe Clark. They honored us with My Little Home in West Virginia.

The calls were all in French, since there were only five people in the village who spoke English. Three of those were us.

It made no difference. The caller changed calls on every dance, but everyone did the same steps over and over. They may not have known two.

They didn't have any West Virginia moon, but they had homemade wine and some clear stuff which burned like moon when you struck a match to it. They took our word on the first round that we didn't drink. Not one insisted. We had a ball.

The wine and clear stuff flowed freely up to a point. I did not see a single person drunk, but they danced hard enough to raise a cloud of dust from the scoured floor. I was an old-timey caller, but I had never heard any of the calls before so we sat out the first two, but when I saw they were doing the same figure all the time, we fell in.

And when I fell out again, I tackled the biggest moose T-bone steak I have ever seen. It was the best shivaree I ever attended.

The Last Piece

This is another story about one of the events that was of major importance at the time and which seemed to be totally ignored by the writers of history of that era. The omission from the annals cannot possibly be because of lack of publicity. I griped about it for weeks afterwards to any and all who would stand in one place long enough for me to get a word or two in slaunchwise.

All of my so-called friends developed a bad habit about that time. They started walking on the opposite side of the road and pulling their caps down over their eyes or pulling their shirt tails up over their faces. As if I wouldn't know who they were anyway!

I told you somewhere else in this book or in one of my other writings (see, I told you my timing belt was slipping) that we were always hungry. That condition seemed to be eternal, even immediately after we had eaten four slices of home baked bread the size of a horseshoe and an inch or more thick, half of a young groundhog, seven boiled and buttered potatoes that were black with pepper, a pint of green beans, a small helping of crock-cured sauerkraut, and two pieces of Mom's apple pie swimming in fresh milk. Full was just a temporary flight of fancy.

Any one of us could have put an Indian warrior to shame except for the fact that all but one of us were just a mite shy of five feet tall at the time. I topped that mark by only a couple inches. The hollow in us went all the way to the ground. That didn't change, regardless of whether we were standing or sitting.

Back in those days, just about everyone owned his own method of transportation. It was attached semi-permanently just below the ankles. The model name was Shank's Mare. The Goodyear tires were attached to the bottoms of the two cows that had been sacrificed to make our shoes. We didn't want cows to go to waste, so we went barefoot as much as possible. The shoes protected your means of locomotion when you wanted to get from here to yonder in cold weather.

Most teachers of that time were only a little better off than the rest of us. If they had forgotten what they had learned in biology class and behind the schoolhouse about cause and effect and had produced a sizeable number of progeny, they were just about able to make ends meet. The ends didn't miss by more than two or three skinny kids.

They had to furnish their own transportation to and from school. For most of them, marriage and subsequent family had denied them sufficient extra funds to purchase a beat-up Model T or Model A, even if there were a few around that could be purchased for less than a hundred dollars if you had also learned to haggle while you were getting classroom credit for time spent behind the building doing biological research.

And while I am just barely on the subject of Henry, I could never figure why he started with a "T." He then went to "A" and then to "B." He stopped right there

235

except for the V-8, which wasn't really a car, just one of the essential parts. Maybe he could foresee the time when he would have more models than he could shake an alphabet at. He may also have foreseen that others would build cars that were much higher in price and much lower in quality and call them by single or multiple letters or by Greek, German, French, Italian, Arabic, and Egyptian Hieroglyphic alphabets and names. The only reason there hasn't been one named in Ogham is that no one knows how to pronounce it and some of the letters look like Kilroy peeping over the fence. World War II veterans will remember Kilroy, who always seemed to get there first.

Most of the teachers I knew traveled by Shank's Mare, just like the rest of us. That helped solve the economic problem and provided part-time employment for poor ignorant younguns like me. The teacher invariably lived at least five miles from school, but always said "Howdy" to the teacher who lived almost next door but taught in the next township when they met in the pasture field on their way to and fro.

The teacher always lived at least twice as far from the school as any of the students. He could hardly ever walk twice as fast. That resulted in considerable lag between up-time and in-time. It was before someone coined the phrase "down-time," so I couldn't use that in this story.

By the time he arrived at the eight-grade one-room school, his legs were not quite ready for running down the long hill to the spring to fetch a pail of water to set on the shelf below the tin dipper that was shared by all and sundry. That was before we knew about those inconveniences called "social diseases," such as AIDS, herpes, and one or two others I'd rather not name.

He wasn't quite up to sweeping and oiling the pine board floor and building a fire in the Burnside pot-bellied stove every morning there was frost on the punkin. He wanted to step from bitter cold into better warmth without walking on a dirty floor. That is where the part-time employment entered the picture.

I always got up before first day light on the first day of school so that I could be first in line to ask for the job. I solemnly swore not to steal any more paper and pencils than was absolutely necessary and not to take blackboard erasers when no one was looking.

I can't recall anyone ever mentioning anything about stealing textbooks. They may have figured those weren't high-risk items, especially when the ambient was full of kids that rarely opened one unless coerced.

All that stuff was furnished by the government, so taking it wasn't really stealing. Not any moreso than stealing food stamps today by either outright theft or by misrepresentation to a willing accomplice, the welfare worker. Nobody but some simple-minded taxpayers have to pay for either.

The job paid top dollar. That was the one that the teacher peeled right off the top of his monthly bank-roll that came in the skinny pay envelope. It was a bargain for both of us, except that I had to carry a key which put a lot of extra weight in my side pocket and more in my cranial cavity because of the responsibility of looking after the other kids who raced to beat the teacher to school. That was when all the fun happened.

That responsibility resulted in the last rubber-hose thrashing that I received in grade school. I got into a fight with an unruly boy only slightly larger than me. It wasn't really a fight. I was sitting on the porch railing with my feet dangling over the outside while I watched the smaller kids playing a game. He came up behind and shoved. I landed on the ground about four feet below on my soft spot. The sudden pressure on the top of my pate and the momentum of my downward plunge combined to cause me to bite a chunk off the end of the only tongue I ever owned.

I jumped up and tore into the culprit to set matters a little more equal. He bled profusely, as the saying goes, and the blood from my mouth was all over his shirt. That was the precise time when the teacher popped around the curve and began to pick up enough speed to qualify him for the Olympic four-hundred.

I completely forgot about my sore mouth when the pain was replaced by one in another location that was rapidly developing huge livid welts from the blows with the hose.

I got my first job of fetching, oiling, sweeping, and firing when I was just past seven years old. I held it by hook and by book through various teachers until I was barely past twelve. One week after my twelfth birthday, I graduated from eighth grade and lost my job because of too much seniority.

I wasn't supposed to go near the school building on weekends except to oil the floors that didn't get done on Friday evening. That came under the heading of useless advice. I could never see any reason to walk the two miles each way to visit a place where I had been imprisoned for more than eight hours a day all week, counting the child-labor time. I made sure the floors were oiled on Friday evening, God willing and the weather permitting, and steered clear of the place until early Monday morning when my routine repeated. Oh, I have walked by a few times on my way 'coon hunting or when looking for a likely fox to chase, but the place was haunted by ghosts of students past and I didn't so much as peek in the windows.

When I started high school that autumn at the ripe old age of twelve, they already had a full-grown man who got there a few years ahead of me and had the job sewed up tight. It was a slightly bigger building and the job paid a little more money.

One of my earlier employers was a female named Leonora McCracken. She doesn't have anything at all to do with this story, but I wanted to mention her anyway. At the risk of being thought redundant, I tell her story in the chapter on Cowboys in my next book, "My Granddaddy Was a Ramblin' Man." I sweet-talked her into coming home with me a couple of times, too. I was seven at the time and still an eligible bachelor. She was somewhere on the short side of twenty-four and still a spinster. I had fallen head-over-heels in love with her a few years earlier but could never squooch up enough courage to tell her how much. She must have known.

I am not sure of the reason for my continuing affection for her. It may have been her radiant personality, her glowing inner beauty, or a new green and tan Model A. It may have been some of all three. She did let me ride in the sedan a few times--in the front seat, with the other passengers in the back.

It didn't work out. She got transferred and I got trapped in my job. I have heard that your first love never dies. I can't respond to that in absolute honesty, because I'm still writing.

Someone once told me that some guy by the name of Fred Something-or-other once said that all love was based on sex. That one wasn't. As far as I was concerned, at least. I wasn't old enough to know much about it except through hearsay, but I had heard plenty said, some of which was pretty hard to believe. She was too old to care--as far as I was concerned, at least. I have vowed never to read one of that guy's books for fear that I might learn something I would rather not know. I have a sneaking suspicion that he may have come from a disoriented and disturbed family.

She was the last woman teacher that I had in grade school. The two men who succeeded her were pretty good and one of them got the credit for getting me out of elementary and into high school, but it wasn't quite the same after she left. I did manage to squeak by in my job, although my heart was somewhere else.

The teacher who was there during my seventh and eighth grades is the real participant in this chapter. It was he who played the leading role and was somewhat responsible for the outcome. That statement may be stretching a point a little since there were several other people, most of them kinfolk, and a few other factors involved.

That male teacher lived about six miles from school. That is as the foot flies and if you cut through a few cow pastures, one bull pasture, climbed several barbed-wire fences, and unhitched three or four contrary gates. Back then it was O.K. to trespass--as long as you followed a few cardinal rules, like closing gates behind you if you found them closed, not teasing the bull, and repairing any fence you didn't clear while jumping.

That was before contingent-fee lawyers evolved and started collecting millions of dollars in damages when you sailed over a barbed-wire fence not quite high enough and ripped the seat of your bib overalls about four layers deep. Patches are not in fashion like they were then, so they cause untold mental anguish to both the rippor and the rippee.

Back then we just laughed if some bare meat happened to be exposed. Every male person of my close acquaintance had been ridiculed at least once. I had

241

been through it more than twice. Today, the only person who can afford to laugh is the lawyer who sort of snickers behind his hand while he is on his way to make a big deposit to his retirement account.

I happened to incur a ripping good time to the seat of a brand new pair of whipcords when I misjudged the height of a barbed-wire fence which happened to get between me and my girl friend's domicile. It may have been that I didn't put enough spring into my spring.

I had to wait in the bedroom with my lower parts clad only in my long-johns while she darned the slit seat so we could talk without her being overly red. Sue? Heck, no! Her name wasn't even close to Sue.

It was common for kids to spend a night now and then with another student. In retrospect, it may have been to get something different to eat.

It was also common practice in those days for the kids to ask the teacher to spend the night with them. That usually happened when the snow was deep enough to strike you between your ankle and another place somewhat higher. That made walking difficult and fence-jumping nigh on to impossible. The teacher was glad to have the opportunity to stay a bit closer to his job and save a dollar or two on his household grub. It was easier to walk on dirt roads that had been partially opened than to break your own trail across the fields.

We had more pull than some of the other kids because there were five of us in school at the same time and we had something like nine uncles in the vicinity who had a reputation for being meaner than a keg of snakes and took insults to the family seriously.

We had singly and collectively invited the teacher to stay over at our house. It was only two miles away and all down hill after a hard day with upwards of twenty unruly brats who ranged in age from about six to one who was full-grown and nineteen years old. The temptation was too great. He quickly made arrangements to stay the next week.

There were a couple of advantages to setting the date for Thursday night, especially if you had been smart enough to ask on Monday of the previous week. One of the most important was connected with child psychology. We knew how to apply it even if we couldn't fathom why there was a "p" in front. The rest of the letters were more of a mystery and none of us learned their proper sequence until several years later. Some of us quit trying.

The interval between the asking and the acceptance gave us a brief respite from switches, corners, etc. He probably felt guilty about applying his board to our seat of learning while waiting to partake of ours.

The big evening finally arrived and with it the teacher, surrounded by all five of us kids who were hoping for a little extra kindness when papers were graded. There is an unsavory term applied to such activity today. If it was back then, I wasn't aware of it. And besides, not too many kids our age wanted to jump on to all five of us. No intelligent parent would want to jump on to all nine of our uncles who had some reputation for being a little on the rough side. Most were careful about what they called us and usually wore a big grin that was probably artificial when they did say something that wasn't really complimentary nor funny. We fought like cats and dogs among ourselves, but we united against any common enemy in the form of an outsider. All the other kids took their turns anyway.

We were as poor as Job's turkey, but we had food. Some of it did grow on trees, as the saying goes, but we had to dig a lot of it out of the ground and pluck a goodly quantity from vines covered with thorns and full of snakes. The hissers knew us on a first-name basis and skeedaddled when they heard us coming.

We also were polite to our guests. I often wonder if we didn't carry that custom a little to far.

We had one other glaring fault. We expected our guests to sit down to a meal that was a bit out of the ordinary for us. My mother was a top-notch country cook and her reputation as a culinary artist spread far and wide. We frequently had guests who just dropped by for a bite. Most of those came unannounced until just in time for Mom to run out and run down a hapless hen or two, whack off their heads with a hatchet she kept near the back door for such emergencies, stick them in the pot and throw in a few extra potatoes. See there, you thought I didn't know how to spell it, didn't you? I will admit that most of those unexpected guests were related by blood or marriage or both, but they were still guests.

That particular evening was no exception. Mom had pilfered a home-cured ham from our smokehouse and had sliced and fried the whole thing except the hock. I told you earlier that we ate--by the bushel.

I sat at the teacher's right in the second place of honor. I was two years nearer to graduating than anyone else and needed all the help I could muster--sometimes spelled "p-u-l-l" and hardly ever spelled "p-u-s-h." I put into practice all my carefully administered upbringing.

I picked up the heaping plate of ham and handed it first to the teacher, just as I had been taught to do. It smelled delicious and the slices were done just right. My salivary glands started doing double-time.

It was a good thing that I did get to smell it. That was as close as I got to the ham. Three or four extra uncles had smelled it from three miles away and had hot-footed it to our house just in time to get their knees under the table. That threw all of Mom's accurate calculations and careful rationing out of kilter. They were lucky enough to pick chairs that were located between the starting gate and the finish line as that plate of hog hip went around the table at a full gallop. Just before it hit the tape, the last piece landed on the plate next to mine. My disappointment was patent.

That last plop has haunted me all my life. I think it psyched my psyche. I still come in on the tail end of just about everything I do. The only consolation I had was that the psychology paid off. I did graduate from elementary school at the top of my class. That may have been helped by the fact that the nineteen year old dropped out about a month before school ended and left me with the eighth grade all to myself.

Historians missed that one, too. They were too preoccupied with unimportant things like bread lines, soup kitchens, starving people, and a funny little wart on the bulging nose of humanity over in Germany who was beginning to make some crazy noises that sounded like trouble was brewing. He was saying nasty things about people who weren't of Aryan ancestry. He even said a couple of nasty things about some who were.

The squeaks of protest from some snot-nosed kid were lost in the uproar. What did it matter that I had to fill my belly with mashed potatoes swimming in hog-grease gravy, home-baked bread, home grown and canned green beans, real cow butter, and sweet potato pie with the bourbon and brandy left out because Mom wanted at least one tee-totaler in the family. She had her hopes pinned on me. Ham be hanged, even if a couple of the uncles did get two pieces.